What's Up in Science?

Puzzles and Problem-Solving Activities to Build Science Literacy, Grades 6–10

Robert G. Hoehn

JOSSEY-BASS
A Wiley Imprint
www.josseybass.com

Jossey-Bass books and products are available through most bookstores. To contact Jossey-Bass directly call our Customer Care Department within the U.S. at 800-956-7739, outside the U.S. at 317-572-3986, or fax 317-572-4002.

Jossey-Bass also publishes its books in a variety of electronic formats. Some content that appears in print may not be available in electronic books.

ISBN 0-7879-7003-4

FIRST EDITION
PB Printing   10 9 8 7 6 5 4 3 2 1

About the Author

Robert G. Hoehn has taught science in California's Roseville Union High School District since 1963. He has received seven National Summer Science Grants from the National Science Foundation and has given numerous presentations to teachers and administrators at local and state science conventions, workshops, and seminars. He also served as a mentor teacher in his district. Mr. Hoehn has a bachelor's degree from San Jose State University and an administrative credential from California State University, Sacramento. He has published a number of nonfiction books and numerous magazine articles. He is currently teaching at Roseville's Independence High School and was named Roseville Area Outstanding Teacher for 2004.

Acknowledgments

Thanks to Christie Hakim, associate editor, for her insight and guidance.

The Standard-Based Concepts included with each activity come from the National Science Education Standards, grades 5 through 12 (Chapter 6), 2002.

*To my wife, Peggy, for her continual help and
support in this effort.*

*To my granddaughter, Shannon Georges, for
her excellent artwork.*

Contents

Section 3: Getting to Know the Lithosphere

Section 4: Listening to the Environment

Section 5: Ocean Features and Related Creatures

Section 6: What's Happening in Space?

Section 7: Life on Land and Water

Section 8: What's Up in Genetic Science?

Section 9: Timely Real-Life Topics of Concern

Introduction

What's Up in Science? offers the busy teacher, grades 6 through 10, current information from recent discoveries and events in science from around the world.

This ready-to-use supplementary resource provides upper elementary, middle school, and general secondary science educators with a variety of activities. These activities quickly engage students in the learning process. Right from the start, they receive a mental challenge: to solve a problem or a puzzle or answer an open-ended question using their creative and critical thinking skills.

What's Up in Science? includes ninety-one activities broken down as follows:

- Section 1: Preserved Evidence of Past Life (twelve activities);
- Section 2: Early Human Life on Earth (six activities);
- Section 3: Getting to Know the Lithosphere (eleven activities);
- Section 4: Listening to the Environment (eight activities);
- Section 5: Ocean Features and Related Creatures (seventeen activities);
- Section 6: What's Happening in Space? (twelve activities);
- Section 7: Life on Land and Water (ten activities);
- Section 8: What's Up in Genetic Science? (eight activities); and
- Section 9: Timely Real-Life Topics of Concern (seven activities).

At the end of each section is a list of challenging activities. They provide an opportunity for students to earn extra credit.

Finally, there is a short section at the end of the book titled Riddles for the Asking. These "mind twisters" will offer an incentive for students to examine the light, humorous side of science.

In the past few years there have been a large number of reported events and discoveries in oceanography, astronomy, and genetic science. Sections 5, 6, and 8 present thirty-seven activities related to these areas of study.

What's Up in Science? provides a mix of challenging problems, puzzles, and open-ended questions to supplement the regular day's work. All activities conclude with Brain Builders, mini-exercises designed to stimulate the creative thinker.

This supplementary teaching resource benefits you, the educator, in the following ways:

- It provides a variety of activities for immediate classroom use.

- It offers current information regarding scientific discoveries and events.

- The activities serve as openers when introducing scientific units and themes.

- The activities center around standard-based concepts.

- The activities make excellent homework assignments, enrichment exercises, or opportunities for students to earn extra credit.

What's Up in Science? assists the learner in the following manner:

- The activities involve real-life events. They provide fresh, relevant information designed to grab and hold the attention of students.

- The activities offer a relaxing, wholesome approach to learning.

- Many of the activities will challenge the creative thinking ability of students. The open-ended questions are at the heart of a science program. These give students an opportunity to freely express their ideas and opinions.

- The activities are broken down into short, intense exercises.

- Students will realize that science is an ongoing process geared to raise more questions than answers.

What's Up in Science? supplies you with a diversity of activities tailored to activate the thinking process and stimulate learning.

Robert G. Hoehn
Independence High School
Roseville, California

Preserved Evidence of Past Life

This section offers twelve activities related to the discovery of fossils. Fossils are the preserved evidence of past geological life. The remains of ancient plants and animals tell a great deal about their surroundings and the conditions under which they lived.

The puzzle exercises, open-ended questions, and brain builder activities in this section are designed to encourage students to use their creative and critical thinking skills. At the end of this section you will find a list titled Challenge Activities. These may serve as a reward for those students who desire extra credit.

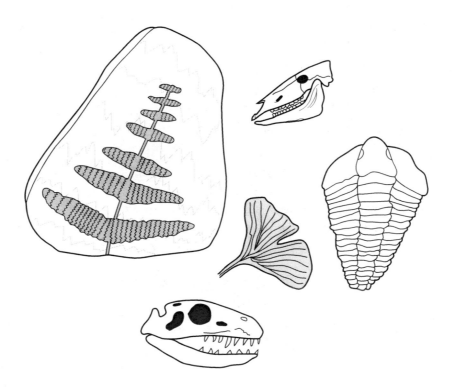

1 What Fossils Have to Say

——Standard–Based Concept——

Fossils provide evidence of how life and environmental conditions have changed.

FOSSIL TALK

Fossils are preserved evidence of ancient geologic life. Ancient geologic life extends from the earliest ages recorded in rocks through the last Ice Age. A fossil may be an insect trapped in amber or a leaf imprint in a layer of sandstone. A saber-toothed cat, preserved in asphalt, and a woolly mammoth, frozen in ice, are examples of fossils. A scientist who studies fossils is known as a paleontologist.

What can be learned from studying fossils? Some reveal their shape, size, and where they lived; others tell a great deal about the conditions under which they lived. Regardless of what fossils say, one thing is clear: Certain plants and animals lived during past ages and then became extinct.

BIG SURPRISE

In 2000, a fisherman in Southern California spotted the fossilized remains of a 25-million-year-old organism thought to be an evolutionary link between a modern organism and its ancient ancestor.

1. Use the clues to help you identify the mystery organism. CLUES: a mammal; a fluke-powered, plankton-eater; three of the letters spell law. *Answer:* _____

2. A paleontologist visited the site and collected parts of the skull and a tooth. He found a third bone. What was it? CLUE: The letters spelling the answer appear in these two words: one, bare. *Answer:* _____

3. Now it's your turn to find fossil animal bones. Let's say you discover four fossil bones while hiking in the hills. In order to receive credit for your find, you must write the bone names in spaces below the sketch. The groups of letters needed to spell the name of each bone are scattered along the hill. Place the bone names in alphabetical order. CLUE: Look for the names of the collarbone, thigh bone, kneecap, and breastbone.

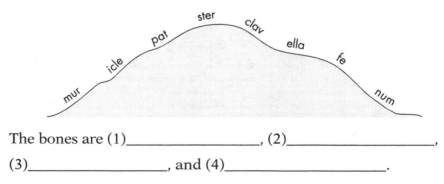

The bones are (1)_____, (2)_____,

(3)_____, and (4)_____.

PASS THE CHEESE

In 2001, a tiny skull reported to be 195 million years old turned up in China. Some scientists believe the organism could be an ancestor to humans. What kind of animal are the scientists talking about?

4. Unscramble five of the eight underlined letters below to reveal the answer. NOTE: Read the material below for a clue as well as pulling out the letters.

Big <u>b</u>rain, co<u>m</u>plex sk<u>u</u>ll

P<u>r</u>obably ate bugs and worm<u>s</u>

Ha<u>d</u> canin<u>e</u>-like tee<u>t</u>h.

The animal was a _____.

BRAIN BUILDERS

Challenge Number One: What do you think this means?

| 0 degrees Centigrade | Age | 32 degrees Fahrenheit |

Challenge Number Two: Plants grow in soil. Think of a way to get soil out of a fossil plant.

2 Long-Ago Life Forms

——Standard–Based Concept——

Scientists rely on fossils to provide evidence about Earth's past.

STARTING POINT

A slow-moving snail. A thorn-covered rosebush. A jellyfish drifting in the sea. These are examples of multi-cellular or many-celled organisms. Some live on land; others prefer a watery environment. And according to one theory, the multi-cellular organisms have been on Earth for 500 million years. A recent fossil find suggests the evolution of multi-cellular life forms may have started a billion years ago.

ONLY A TRACE

Scientists in India have found what appear to be tunnels left by prehistoric animals. They found the burrows in 1.1 billion-year-old rocks. There were no remains of the tunnel-digging creatures. The fossilized tunnels are known as trace fossils. A trace fossil provides evidence that a once-living organism lived there but left no remains behind. Even so, scientists study trace fossils and gain valuable information about prehistoric life.

1. What sort of animals can you think of that might dig tunnels?

2. Scientists believe the tunnels are twice as old as any other evidence for multi-cellular life yet discovered. What evidence might support this condition?

WHAT DO YOU KNOW ABOUT WORMS?

Some scientists think wormlike creatures tunneled through sand beds underneath a shallow sea covering what is now central India. Since no remains exist, scientists can't say for sure what these ancient organisms looked like. However, we do know a few things about modern-day squirmy worms.

3. Let's test your worm I.Q. Use the clues to help you complete the puzzle.

W _ _ _ _ _   a worm's short, jerky motion

O _ _ _ _ _ _   a worm's internal structures

R _ _ _ _   some worms have this body shape

M _ _ _ _ _   these worms live in the sea

S _ _ _   where some worms live

4. Look at the tunnels labeled A, B, and C in the illustration below. What do you notice about the diameter of the burrow holes?

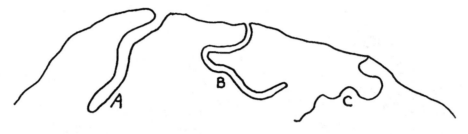

I noticed the burrow holes _____

_____

If you noticed that Tunnel A was much wider than Tunnel B, that will help you understand why scientists assume that the longer a tunnel was used by the organisms, the wider it became.

BRAIN BUILDERS

Challenge Number One: Think of a way to illustrate a WIDE tunnel using six letters and five dashes.

Challenge Number Two: Gophers are burrowing rodents. They leave holes or openings in the ground. What four letters in GOPHER spell a name that describes a small opening?

3 Footprints from the Past

──Standard-Based Concept──

Organisms become preserved as fossils in a variety of ways.

FOSSIL TALK

Fossils are preserved evidence of past ancient life. Scientists find many fossil bones, shells, and teeth in different parts of the world. These hard parts may stay buried for millions of years and undergo little change.

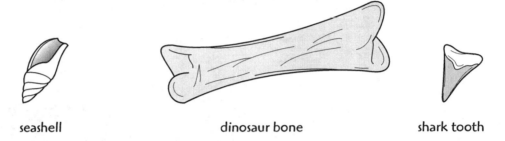

seashell   dinosaur bone   shark tooth

Paleontologists are scientists who study plant and animal fossils. Many fossils reveal secrets about life in the past, such as climate and environmental conditions. Most fossils are found in sedimentary rock.

MORE FOSSIL GOSSIP

Not all fossils come from the hard parts of organisms. Animal footprints, worm burrows, and trails of animals may harden as a mold. A mold is a cavity or imprint left by an organism. In time the mold becomes buried under layers of sedimentary material.

STEP BY STEP

In April 2000, a man in St. George, Utah, found about 150 dinosaur footprints in his backyard. Scientists say the footprints are representative of a mix of plant- and meat-eating dinosaurs that lived about 200 million years ago.

1. Read the statements below. Then arrange them in the order you think best describes how dinosaur footprints might turn into fossils. Write the statements in the empty spaces.

   - They plod through mud and leave footprints behind.
   - They seek food along a river bank or lake shoreline.
   - Layers of mud, clay, or rock build up over the prints.
   - A mixture of sand and water covers the prints.
   - Millions of years pass by.
   - Several dinosaurs are present.

Footprints from the Past *(continued)*

- Fossilized footprints form in sedimentary rock.
- The mixture turns into cement and hardens.
- They step in soft mud and sink.

(1) _____

(2) _____

(3) _____

(4) _____

(5) _____

(6) _____

(7) _____

(8) _____

(9) _____

2. What do you think dinosaur footprints tell scientists?

3. Circle the four parts of a foot hiding in the series of letters that could easily be identified in a fossil footprint.

   o c r a n i n s t e p h e e l t o r i d c l a w e t o l t o e b y a k l e

4. If you discovered fossil tracks like those below, what would you say the animal was doing?

BRAIN BUILDERS

Challenge Number One: What four letters in DINOSAUR spell the name of rock material finer than gravel?

Challenge Number Two: Five letters in DINOSAUR spell radio. If you take a DINOSAUR's radio away, the remaining letters would spell the name of a star in the solar system. What is the name of the star?

4 Early Wings

──Standard-Based Concept──

Scientists base their explanations of nature using observations, experiments, and a variety of scientific models. These interpretations are tentative and subject to change.

SCIENCE IS . . .

The process of science is based on producing knowledge about the physical world. A scientist may collect evidence by observing a subject over time or by gathering data from technical sources. Although much information has been collected over the years, many natural processes and events remain a mystery.

MAYBE OR MAYBE NOT

Many scientists believe birds evolved from dinosaurs. Fossils found in central Asia in 1969 by a Russian scientist have recently come under study. The fossils show a feathered reptile from about 220 million years ago. Surprisingly, this would be 75 million years BEFORE the first bird.

1. Does the fossil evidence prove that birds evolved from an earlier reptile rather than a dinosaur? Why or why not?

2. The fossil evidence indicates that the early reptile lacked the muscles needed for flight. If so, what might have been the function of the feathers?

3. According to the findings, the teeth and various body structures of the fossil remains are like those of birds. Is this enough evidence to say that birds evolved from earlier reptiles? Why or why not?

Early Wings (continued)

SHERLOCK BONES

A paleontologist is a fossil scientist who, like a detective, gathers information to solve problems. A paleontologist often has to determine past events from a limited amount of evidence. Here's your chance to play Fossil Detective. Use the clues to help you solve the following problems:

4. Dr. Jennifer Ortiz, paleontologist, found an extinct amphibian bone. Name the bone and tell where it belongs in the animal's body. Fill in the blanks with the answers. Use the clues to help you find the answers.

   CLUE: A straight line from the center of a circle to the surface.

   CLUE: Not in the head or the pelvic zone. Try what lies next to the ulna bone.

   The __ a __ __ __ s is found in the _____.

5. Dr. Lewis Means, paleontologist, uncovered an extinct reptile bone. Name the bone and tell where it belongs in the animal's body. Fill in the blanks with the answers.

   CLUE: Rearrange these groups of letters: le dib man

   CLUE: It rests below the eyes and nose, and serves to rip its deadly foes.

   The __ __ n __ __ __ l __ is found in the _____.

BRAIN BUILDERS

Challenge Number One: The feathered, four-legged reptile was 83 percent of one foot long. How long is that in inches?

Challenge Number Two: Use four letters in FOSSIL to describe the surface layer of earth.

5 Two Steps Ahead of the Rest

——Standard-Based Concept——

Fossils indicate that many organisms living long ago are now extinct. Lizards appeared about 200 million years ago. Some survived extinction and continue to live today.

A LOOK AT LIZARDS

Lizards are reptiles with long, slender, scaly bodies. They travel on four legs and carry a long tail. They live in hot, dry deserts all over the world. Lizards have external (outside) ears and legs with clawed toes on each foot. They can move their eyelids. Lizards measure from 5 cm (about 2 inches) to 12 feet in length. Some legless lizards bear a close resemblance to snakes.

QUARRY TREASURE

In 2000, researchers in Germany found the fossil remains of a new species of lizard. They removed the fossil from a stone quarry. A quarry is a place where rocks are cut or blasted out of an area. The rocks are used for building materials.

1. Why were the researchers lucky to find a new species of lizard in the stone quarry?

2. After the researchers brought the 10-inch fossil to the lab, it took them two years to remove the rock that encased the lizard. Why do you think it took so long?

TWO-LEGGED SURPRISE

The new find amazed the researchers. The remains showed the lizard to be a two-footed sprinter able to outrun the hungriest predator. The ability to walk upright on two feet is known as bipedalism.

3. Many bipeds have long, strong hind legs. This gives them excellent jumping ability and allows them to run at a fast clip. Use this information to complete the drawing of the lizard.

OLDER THAN TIME

4. Scientists use a process called age dating to tell the approximate age of a fossil. They believe the lizard may be _____ million years old. Solve the problem and write the answer in the blank space. PROBLEM: Multiply 5.9 by 60. Add 2,140 to the answer. Subtract 372 from the total. Add 1,400. Now divide the total by 6, then subtract 297. NOTE: This problem is an arithmetic stretching exercise, not a model of age-dating.

THE CLOCK RAN OUT

5. A very fast plant-eating lizard that weighed less than a pound lived among the huge meat-eating reptiles. Can you think of some reasons why its species might have died off before the dinosaurs appeared?

BRAIN BUILDERS

Challenge Number One: Dr. Mary Stiles, scientist, found four fossil bones of a frog in Cooper's Quarry. The bone names rhymed with dreamer, yesterday, lull, and radical. What are the names of the bones?

Challenge Number Two: How could a lizard be changed into hog fat?

6 Dinosaur-Snacking Crocodile

——Standard-Based Concept——

Fossils indicate that many organisms living long ago are now extinct. However, some species of crocodiles have managed to survive for over 200 million years.

CROCODILE PROFILE

A crocodile is a large, meat-eating reptile that lives in or around tropical streams and rivers. Crocodiles have long, slender snouts and are very aggressive. Cone-like teeth line their powerful jaws. These four-limbed reptiles have a thick, scaly skin and carry a heavy tail. Some crocodiles reach a length of over 20 feet.

SUPER CROC

Meet Sarchosuchus, a 40-foot-long crocodile believed to have weighed 17,500 pounds (over 8 tons). In 2000, Dr. Paul Sereno, paleontologist, found fossil bones of the monster reptile in Africa. He called the creature "Super Croc." Dr. Sereno thinks Super Croc used its massive size to explode out of the water to grab and eat dinosaurs.

GONE FOREVER

1. When a species dies out, it becomes extinct. Many species of organisms that lived on Earth no longer exist. What might be some of the reasons Super Croc failed to survive?

FOUR NO MORE

2. In the scattered letters below, circle the letters that spell the names of four extinct dinosaurs that lived around the same time as Super Croc. Answers may be forward and backward. NOTE: There is one name in each of four of the six strings of letters. See the hints below.

D S P O T A R E C I R T I   A S T E G O S A U R U S L

R W O K G N I G D A C Y   B T R I L O B I T E S P A

E B R O N T O S A U R E M   S U R U A S O N N A R Y T

HINTS: (1) The "rex" part of the name is missing. (2) Carries heavy bony plates on its back. (3) A 30-ton reptile. (4) A long horn over each eye, a short horn on the nose. NOTE: The hints are not in any particular order.

TOP CHOICE

3. Why do you think Africa might be a good place to hunt for fossils?

SNIFF, SNIFF

4. The remains of Super Croc revealed a large sinus cavity at the tip of its nose. How do you think this might help an animal survive?

ARM YOURSELF

5. Scutes are outside bony plates found on some fishes and reptiles. The scale-like structures serve as protection against enemies. Super Croc had 18-inch scutes along its back. Dr. Sereno believes the scutes acted like radiators as Super Croc soaked in the sun. How are scutes like solar panels on the roof of a house?

BRAIN BUILDERS

Challenge Number One: What do these letters indicate? SdUiPnEoRs CaRuOrC

Challenge Number Two: If each student is 4'6" tall, how many students lying head to foot would it take to equal the length of Super Croc?

7 Awesome Dinosaur

Standard–Based Concept

Extinction of a species occurs when the environment changes and the adaptive characteristics of a species are insufficient to allow its survival.

RULING REPTILES

Dinosaurs, the ruling reptiles of the Mesozoic Era, lived on Earth for about 160 million years. The term dinosaur means "terrible lizard." These reptiles lived on land and water. The plant-eating dinosaurs used all four limbs to move about, while the meat-eaters depended on their hind legs to overtake prey. Scientists tell us many of the dinosaurs weren't much bigger than a small turkey. Dinosaurs became extinct 65 million years ago.

BRONTO BUSTER

Apatosaurus, also known as Brontosaurus, carried a 35-ton body on four short, elephant-like legs. Its long neck and tail made up most of the animal's length. This plant-eater lived in a swampy habitat during the late Jurassic period, about 160 million years ago. Scientists found several headless Apatosaurus skeletons. Fortunately, after hours of hard work, the scientists were able to assemble complete skeletons of the beast.

1. Draw a head and neck to complete the Apatosaurus sketch. Think about creating a long, flexible neck and a small head.

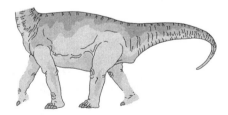

2. The huge plant-eating Apatosaurus carried a one-pound brain to operate a 60,000-pound frame. That's a lot of "beef" to guide through the swamp.

   In the preceding paragraph, circle the hiding places of two insects, one rodent, and a male sheep.

3. Apatosaurus shook the ground as it walked. Scientists called it the " _ _ _ _ _ _ _ reptile." Use seven of the scattered letters to fill the spaces. HINT: The answer rhymes with blunder and plunder.

   n e h z   s t r u   i d e

   Use the remaining four letters to complete this sentence: The _ _ _ _ of the Apatosaurus may have protected it from meat-eating dinosaurs.

4. Can you imagine how many pounds an animal as big as Apatosaurus might gain in one day? Scientists analyzed fossil leg bones to reveal the answer. They reported the giant reptile gained more than _____ pounds a day at the peak of its growth spurt. After you solve the following problem, you'll have an answer for the space above. NOTE: This is an arithmetic problem, not a way that scientists actually calculate size.

   a. Multiply a dozen by one-half of five.
   b. Add 60 to the answer from Step (a).
   c. Divide the answer from Step (b) by a trio.

5. Suppose the average growth spurt lasted 3.5 months. How many pounds would Apatosaurus gain during this time? Apatosaurus would gain _____ pounds.

BRAIN BUILDERS

Challenge Number One: Think of a way to show how the following numbers and letters combine to read: "Extinction is forever."

   Sn   c   (2+2)   is   x   ever   shun

CLUE: Look for a chemical symbol to help you reveal the answer.

Challenge Number Two: Huge, enormous, and mighty are words used to describe a dinosaur of size and strength. Use 5 letters from those words to create an adjective to describe a tiny reptile.

8 Even More Dinosaurs

Standard-Based Concept

Fossils indicate that many organisms that lived long ago are now extinct. Many of the species that have lived on Earth no longer exist.

ROMP IN THE SWAMP

Once upon a time (late Jurassic) a swamp monster known as Brachiosaurus held the title of largest animal of all time. This 40-ton beast boasted a seven-foot humerus (upper "arm" bone), a 28-foot-long neck, and ribs measuring over eight feet in length. Brachiosaurus stood 40 feet high and reached a length of 80 feet.

Brachiosaurus spent most of the time in large bodies of water. The water helped buoy the animal's weight so it could lumber about in search of food. The beast's slow movement and limited brainpower made it an easy target for flesh-eating dinosaurs.

BRAIN STRAIN

1. The human brain weighs about three pounds. A person weighing 180 pounds has a brain that makes up approximately 1.7 percent of his or her body weight (180 pounds divided into 3 pounds). A 40-ton Brachiosaurus had a 7-ounce brain. What percent of its body weight is made up of brain tissue? HINT: 16 ounces = one pound; 2,000 pounds = 1 ton.

BYE-BYE BRACHIOSAURUS

2. Mass extinction of dinosaurs occurred about 65 million years ago. Most scientists agree a _____ _____ killed them off. Unscramble the following letters for the answer. (First word: grela. Second word: teemotire.)

FLESH-EATING MACHINE

Farmers in the Argentine Patagonia area in South America recently found fossilized bones of the largest meat-eating dinosaurs found so far. They showed their find to a local paleontologist. Details of the remains revealed a 45-foot-long reptile that weighed around 18,000 pounds. It could swallow a person in one bite.

3. Scientists say the beast never tasted human flesh. What might be the reason for this?

The new discovery falls into the reptile group known as theropods. Theropods walked on three birdlike toes and were flesh-eaters.

4. Create a sketch in the space below of how you think a theropod's footprint might appear in sand or mud.

MORE TO COME

The Argentine Patagonia is a dry, grassy region in the northern part of Argentina. Recently this desert bush country provided scientists with one of the largest dinosaurs ever found. The plant-eating monster weighed 100 tons.

5. What name did they give to the animal? Put the scattered letters in their proper order for the answer. HINT: In what country did they find the dinosaur?

ur   tin   Ar   osa   gen   us

The name of the reptile is __ __ __ e __ __ __ __ __ o __ a __ __ __ __

BRAIN BUILDERS

Challenge Number One: Use EVERY letter in DINOSAUR to spell the answers to these questions:

a. What do you call examples of noise and tone?

b. What substance carries a noise or tone?

Challenge Number Two: What three letters in MESOZOIC (geologic era) spell a name to describe a collection of wild animals?

9 Mast from the Past

—Standard-Based Concept—

Extinction of a species occurs when the environment changes and it fails to survive.

MASTODON IN TOWN

In 2001, a teenage boy from Garnerville, Nevada, discovered the fossilized bones of a North American mastodon. A mastodon is an elephant-like beast with tusks and a long trunk. According to scientists, the mammal may have lived between 5 million and 23 million years ago.

MAMMALS EVERYWHERE

Scientists say the North American mastodon lived among horses, antelopes, camels, and bears. It had to defend itself against such predators as wolves and large cats.

1. In the figure below, shade in two things scientists think the mastodon used against its enemies.

ANCIENT PARADISE

2. Scientists described the area where the Mastodon lived as a golden age for large mammals. They believed the _____ allowed for lush _____ and plenty of _____ and _____. Combine the groups of letters below to form the words needed to fill the empty spaces.

od	ter
cli	grass
land	fo
mate	wa

3. Once the news of a fossil find reaches the community, the discovery site needs to be protected from intruders. What things do you think need to be done to protect the site?

DREAM SCHEME

The descriptions of organisms below represent extinct animals. Let's pretend that scientists discover living specimens of these creatures. How many of them do you recognize?

4. Test your knowledge by writing the name of the animals in the empty spaces. HINT: The names are scattered below.

Woolly mammoth	Triceratops	Stegosaurus
Plesiosaurus	Saber-toothed cat	Trilobite

- Lion-like massive body; curved, knife-like canine teeth:

  _____

- Dinosaur-like, 25 feet long, 10 feet high, long horn above each eye, short horn on the nose: _____

- Crab-like sea creature; three-lobed body: _____

- Elephant-like; long, curved tusks, hairy skin:

  _____

- Marine reptile, about 10 feet long, long neck, oar-like legs and feet:

  _____

- Twenty-three feet long; many teeth; leathery skin, and bony plates along the neck, back, and tail: _____

BRAIN BUILDERS

Challenge Number One: Find three letters in MASTODON that spell a term meaning a unit of weight equal to 2,000 pounds.

Challenge Number Two: Find three letters in MASTODON that spell a term identifying a member of the primate family.

10 North American Mammal Mystery

——Standard–Based Concept——

Human activities harm certain living species through population growth, pollution, and overuse and abuse of natural resources.

MAMMAL MELODRAMA

In 2001, a news report came out stating that about fifty-three large North American mammals disappeared from Earth in the last 10,000 years. What happened to them? One theory suggests ancient Stone Age travelers from Asia came into North America about 11 thousand years ago. According to the theory, the invaders may have hunted most of the large mammals to extinction.

1. What evidence would you like to examine before deciding whether or not to accept the theory?

LINE 'EM UP

2. Connect the letter or letters from lines 1, 2, and 3 to spell the names of eight North American mammals. Begin at the top of line 1 and go from left to right.

(1)	(2)	(3)
ma	e	l
c	r	h
ca	sto	se
ma	mm	don
sl	av	oth
be	me	er
b	ot	ar
ho	a	t

Write the names of the mammals in the spaces below.

a. _____   e. _____

b. _____   f. _____

c. _____   g. _____

d. _____   h. _____

What's Up in Science?

SPARE A THOUGHT

Write what you think about each of the following statements:

3. Whales and seals have been over-hunted for years. Some people say over-hunting leads to extinction. Why do you think whales and seals manage to survive?

4. Extinction in the Americas seems to follow the arrival of humans. If humans are responsible for the disappearance of large North American mammals, then why do you think there are large North American mammals living today?

MAYBE THIS HAPPENED . . .

5. Another theory states a __ __ __ __ __ __ __ brought in by ancient settlers may have caused widespread __ __ __ __ __ __ __ __. Perhaps a plague may have wiped out the animals. All the letters needed to fill the empty spaces are in the statement: Rob said, "See mice." HINT: The first answer is another name for germ; the second answer rhymes with cheese and sneeze.

BRAIN BUILDERS

Challenge Number One: What is the sketch saying about mammal extinction?

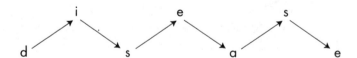

Challenge Number Two: What is the sketch saying about causes of mammal extinction?

11 Fossils on Hold

—Standard-Based Concept—

Fossils provide evidence of how life and environmental conditions have changed. Some species of plants and animals continue to survive and show little change over millions of years.

ALIVE AND SWIMMING

A living fossil is an organism believed to be extinct or nearly extinct, but that continues to live on Earth. For example, a prehistoric fish known as a coelacanth lived between 100 and 200 million years ago. In 1938, a fisherman caught one off the coast of Africa. Recently another fisherman from Indonesia, 6,000 miles west of Africa, caught a four-foot long, 64-pound coelacanth.

1. The coelacanth has an unusual tail or caudal fin. The thick tail has three sections, including a distinctive fin that protrudes from the middle. Complete the sketch of the coelacanth by drawing a tail matching the description.

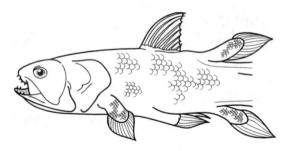

KEEPING A LOW PROFILE

2. Scientists believed the coelacanth had been extinct for 65 million years. In fact, the coelacanth lived in the __ __ __   __ __   __ __ __ __ __ __ __ __ __ __. The words needed to fill the spaces are hidden in the series of letters below. Find them and write the letters in the blanks.

    CLUE:

    > Ten letters name this scaly creature,
    >
    > Line them out and please your teacher,
    >
    > The remaining letters hold the key.
    >
    > So go left to right and then you'll see.
    >
    > C O E A G E L A C O F D I N O A N S A T H U R S

PLANT: PAST AND PRESENT

This plant is a great example of a living fossil. The Chinese held it as a sacred tree in temple gardens since ancient times. The Chinese enjoy roasting and eating the seeds of the plant. The mystery plant grows in parks, along city streets, and in residential areas. The plant is the only species of its kind that still survives from the Age of Dinosaurs.

3. Identify the mystery living fossil from the following three clues:

   a. Six letters in name: n g i k o g

   b. The name rhymes with "stink-o"

   c. The plant has fan-shaped leaves

   The living fossil plant is a _____.

STROMATOLITE DELIGHT

Stromatolites are examples of living fossils. The fossil forms exist as algae reefs from the Precambrian Era, 3 BILLION YEARS AGO. Stromatolites are alternating thin layers of silt mixed with calcium carbonate made by blue-green algae. They produce wave-like or rounded shapes. Living stromatolites in Western Australia closely resemble the fossil remains from the Precambrian Era.

4. Calcium carbonate, $CaCO_3$, is a mineral found in limestone and marble. $CaCO_3$ is a molecule made up of three elements, calcium (Ca), carbon (C), and Oxygen (O_2). See how many calcium carbonate molecules you can make from the elements below.

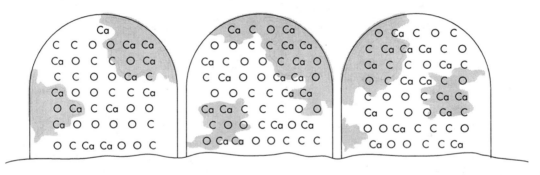

There are _____ calcium carbonate molecules.

BRAIN BUILDERS

Challenge Number One: What needs to happen before an organism can become a living fossil?

Challenge Number Two: According to Webster, an oxymoron is a figure of speech in which opposite or contradictory ideas or terms are combined. Example: Joe's in a slow rush. Is the term "living fossil" an oxymoron? Why or why not?

12 Let's Ban Man

Standard-Based Concept

Human activities harm certain living species through population growth, pollution, and overuse and abuse of natural resources.

DOOM AND GLOOM

A 2000 report from the World Conservation Union's Red List of Threatened Species predicts over 11 thousand plants and animals may soon vanish from the earth. Many living species are identified as critically endangered or close to extinction.

1. The events responsible for the high extinction rate appear below. Fill in the blanks with the missing letters.

$$\_\,H\,\_\,\_\,i\,c\,\_\,\_\;poisoning$$

$$over\_\,\_\,\_\,U\,l\,\_\,t\,\_\,\_\,\_$$

$$poor\;M\,\_\,n\,\_\,\_\,em\,\_\,nt$$

$$increased\;p\,\_\,A\,c\,\_\,\_\,ng\;(rhymes\;with\;coaching)$$

$$lack\;of\;\_\,Nt\,\_\,\_\,\_\,st$$

$$over\,\_\,\_\,S\,\_\,\_\,ng$$

WIPED OUT

Extinction occurs when a living species, plant or animal, dies out. The organism is no longer active or in existence.

2. Find and circle three extinct organisms listed below. CLUE: The right answers will have hidden words in them, meaning a butterfly-like insect, hog or swine, and sharp-edged sword.

coelacanth   saber-tooth cat   gingko   royal palm   Manx cat   pectin
bulbet fern   white pelican   chukar   passenger pigeon   woolly mammoth
horsetail   avocado   New Jersey hamster   grouse   humpback whale

NO MO DODO

A large, flightless dodo bird from the island of Mauritius (Indian Ocean) lives no more. The slow-moving bird became extinct in the late 1600s. Several factors combined to send the bird to a speedy end.

3. _____ _____ ate dodo eggs and contributed to the bird's extinction. The figure of the dodo bird contains scattered groups of letters. Put them together and place the two-word answer in the empty spaces.

ONE TOO MANY

A threatened species experiences possible harm or evil. Scientists say around 816 species have disappeared in the last 500 years.

4. What do you think it means when scientists refer to species being at "significant risk"?

BRAIN BUILDERS

Challenge Number One: Use four letters in EXTINCTION to spell a word meaning "going out" or departure.

Challenge Number Two: Endangered means subject to loss or injury. What three letters in ENDANGERED describe extinction?

Section 1

Preserved Evidence of Past Life: Challenge Activities

1. If fossil remains could speak, they could provide important information to scientists. How do you think a woolly mammoth from the Ice Age might describe the northern environment? Write a three- or four-sentence paragraph on a separate sheet of paper.

2. A pit contained numerous fossilized mammal bones, amphibian bones, and several plant leaf imprints. How would you describe the ancient environment from the fossil remains? Include a sketch with labels in your description.

3. Use two or three paragraphs to describe how a mammal from the Ice Age might become refrigerated.

4. Describe two or three ways an insect might become a fossil.

5. Give several examples of imprint fossils. Explain how a plant leaf becomes an imprint.

6. Explain how the process of metamorphism prevented ancient organisms from becoming fossils. Use illustrations in your description.

7. Select an era of geologic history. Describe the era and list several organisms from the era that became fossils.

8. Describe the "Age of Reptiles" and identify several plants and animals that lived during that time.

9. A paleontologist is a scientist who studies fossils. In what ways might a paleontologist add to the pool of scientific knowledge?

10. Describe three animal organisms and three plant organisms scientists say are living fossils.

Early Human Life on Earth

This section offers six activities dealing with fossil evidence and artifacts regarding primitive human life on Earth. The activities provide students with examples of how life and environmental conditions change over time. Students see the role archaeologists play in making new discoveries in different parts of the world.

The puzzle exercises, open-ended questions, and brain builder activities in this section are designed to encourage students to use their creative and critical thinking skills. At the end of this section you will find a list titled Challenge Activities. These may serve as a reward for those students who desire extra credit.

13 New Face from an Old Skull

—Standard-Based Concept—

The millions of different species of plants, animals, and microorganisms that live on Earth today are related by descent from common ancestors.

HUMAN ORIGINS

Paleontology is the field of science that deals with prehistoric fossil life forms. These forms may be plant or animal. Recent discoveries of fossil bones indicate that early human ancestors appeared on Earth several million years ago. However, scientists can't say for sure when man's common ancestor first appeared on Earth.

OFFERINGS FROM THE CRUST

For several years, a 3.2 million-year-old skeleton called Lucy was believed to be the earliest known human ancestor. In 2001, scientists unearthed a skull with tiny, worn-down teeth. It resembled a modern-looking face. They found the bones in Kenya, Africa. Scientists believe the bone fragments from the mysterious creature are around 3.5 million years old. Could the creature be a link to the human family tree?

1. What kind of food do you think the creature may have eaten? Circle your choices from the following items. HINT: The skull contained tiny, worn-down teeth.

large mammals	fruit	tree roots	insects	tree bark	dried animal skin
shrubs	ground bones	tree branches	dried fish	palm leaves	worms

2. What kind of diet do small teeth indicate?

MORE BONES AHEAD

Scientists reported finding several skull and jaw fragments. They didn't recover any long bones or ribs from the creature's remains.

3. Can you think of a reason why long bones (legs and arms) or rib bones might be missing?

SKULL SESSION

4. Unscramble the names of five features found on the human skull. Then place an X on the sketch where each feature is located.

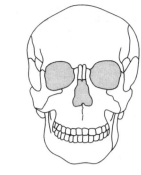

a. teteh _____

b. lrwoe jwa _____

c. ckehe _____

d. ncih _____

e. pruep ajw _____

BONE HERE, BONE THERE

Scientists have found scattered bones from several different individuals in various parts of the world. A mixture of assorted bones makes it impossible to determine an organism's size or appearance. It would be like trying to complete a jigsaw puzzle with three pieces missing.

5. Unscramble the following five bones. Write the name of each bone in the space to the right.

ibr_____ vcelpi _____ muref _____

drlohsue delab _____ _____ hins _____

BRAIN BUILDERS

Challenge Number One: What does the sketch represent?

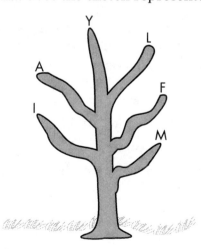

Challenge Number Two: Find and circle two parts of the human body in the following sentence:

Mr. Tee thought he'd scribble a note or two on his writing tablet.

14 Who Ate My Kangaroo?

——Standard-Based Concept——

Environmental conditions have changed. Fossils indicate that many organisms that lived long ago are extinct.

MAMMAL GATHERING

What single word describes humans, horses, and whales? Mammal. Mammals have body hair, a four-chambered heart, and warm blood. Females carry glands that secrete milk as food for their young. Scientists believe mammals evolved from a reptilian ancestor. As the dinosaurs died out about 65 million years ago, the mammal population grew. Mammals remain one of the most successful groups of animals on Earth. As environmental conditions changed over time, some animals became extinct and left fossils for scientists to study.

Some scientists blame early human hunters for the mass extinction of large groups of mammals. Mass extinction refers to large numbers of organisms dying around the same time.

BEAST FEAST

How about a plate of kangaroo stew? Maybe you'd prefer a mammoth burger or cream of ground sloth soup. New studies report that early hunters dined on these animals about 50,000 years ago in Australia and North America. Some scientists believe the disappearance of big mammals and flightless birds occurred around the same time that modern humans appeared. Age dating technology shows the Australian animals vanished just when humans were spreading across the continent. Early man may have eaten too many mammals, but other theories offer additional reasons why mammals disappeared from Earth.

1. Let's say you're an early human hunter with an appetite for the large, flightless emu-like bird running around Australia. If you correctly count the number of times "emu" appears on the dinner menu, you'll eat free for a week.

Early Hunter's Hangout Dinner Menu Specials
- Roast emu femur stuffed with prairie twigs.
- Emu broth emulsion over kangaroo noodles.
- Barbecued lemur-like ribs wrapped in kangaroo pouch

"emu" appears _____ times on the menu.

Who Ate My Kangaroo? *(continued)*

REALLY RESTLESS

According to the findings, it appears the ancient human hunters moved from one region to another.

2. What word describes this type of movement? To find out, circle the letters that spell the names of eight animals living today in Australia. Move from left to right as you circle the letters. Use nine of the circled letters for the answer. (Be careful! One letter is used twice.) HINT: Look for six mammals, one reptile, and one insect.

   E M U A K O A L A B E A R M K A
   N G A R O O I P L A T Y P U S N
   A N T E A T E R G W A L L A B Y
   T R O C R O C O D I L E I A N T

   The nine-letter word is _____.

3. Early hunters ate their fill of North American mammals. Luckily, many animals survived and continued to live in forests and flatlands.

   Fill in the missing letters to identify five animals living in North America today.

   m __ o __ e, h __ r __ e, c __ r __ b __ u, b __ s __ n, s __ e __ p

BRAIN BUILDERS

Challenge Number One: Where might you find "emu" hiding in your favorite restaurant?

Challenge Number Two: Think of a way the force of friction can cause the disappearance of mammals.

15 Early Artists Show Their Skill

—Standard-Based Concept—

Responses to external stimuli can result from interactions with the organism's own species and others, as well as from environmental changes; these responses either can be innate or learned. Scientists are influenced by societal, cultural, and personal beliefs and ways of viewing the world. Science is an important part of society.

EARTH ART

Scientists have discovered numerous wall paintings and engravings created by prehistoric cave dwellers in Spain, France, and other countries. The "cave art" dates from 40,000 to 10,000 years ago. Many of the paintings show animals, geometric signs, and figures depicting life through the eyes of creative primitive people.

X MARKS THE SPOT

In 2001, the earliest known piece of art may have been found in South Africa. Scientists found a flat stone with a series of X marks etched into it. They believe the scratches symbolize something important to the people who made them.

1. Why do you think the meanings of the X marks may never be known?

MODERN-DAY X's

2. The letter X holds value to many people. Here's a chance to test your "X I.Q." Complete each statement by filling in the blanks with the missing letters.

   a. An X is used for playing the game tic-tac-t__ __.

   b. A football coach uses X's and O's to represent p__a__ __r s.

   c. An X indicates a c__ec__ mark for an item on a list.

   d. A person unable to spell his or her __ __ __ __ might place an X in the signature space.

   e. An X or crossbuck sign appears near a r__i__ ro__ __ track.

   f. Students X out unwanted items from their homework p__ __ers.

ART I.Q.

3. Let's test your ability to handle X, the 24th letter of the English alphabet. Sketch a series of X marks on the rock slab.

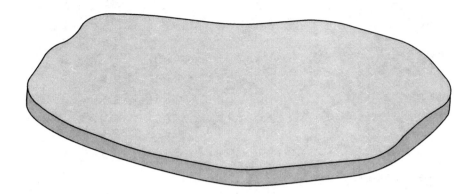

a. Do you think the X's drawn on the rock slab represent art? Why or why not?

b. Why do you think primitive man drew on cave walls and large rocks?

c. What could you learn about early man by studying their art?

HOW OLD IS "X"?

4. Scientists think the flat stone marked with X's may be over _____ thousand years old. Solve the following problem and place the answer in the space above.

(a) 30.0 divided by 2.5; (b) multiply Answer (a) by five; (c) add a dozen to Answer (b); (d) subtract 3 decades from Answer (c); (e) add the total of 6 + 15 + 3 + 4 to Answer (d).

NOTE: This is an arithmetic game, not a scientific calculation method.

BRAIN BUILDERS

Challenge Number One: "Art" helps make up an organ and a vessel in the human body. Name the organ and vessel.

Challenge Number Two: Use the scattered letters to complete the spelling of the term that describes the study of the remains of ancient cultures.

_ _ _ _ _ _ o l o g y

h a c e r a

16 Egyptian Cave Art

——Standard-Based Concept——

Scientific progress is made by asking meaningful questions and conducting careful investigations. Formulating explanations by using logic and evidence is an important part of this process.

EARLY RISERS

The artifacts recovered from early prehistoric dwellers on the Nile indicate a gradual shift from hunting and fishing to farming. The ancient people of the Predynastic period (4000 to 3100 B.C.) created "cemetery art." This was art produced for the dead to use in the afterlife. Decorated pottery, figurines, tools, and weapons were placed in the grave with the body. This would keep the spirit in the next life well-supplied with goods.

MODERN OR ANCIENT ART?

Recently a man hunting for fossils in the Egyptian desert found cave drawings. At first some experts thought the art might date back to 7000 B.C. Now a leading Egyptologist believes the drawings are imitations or fakes no more than twenty years old.

1. What did the experts FIRST see to grab and hold their attention? Arrange the underlined letters in the statement below to spell the answer.

   P r e h i s t o r i c   d w e l l e r s   o n   t h e   N i l e

2. The experts decided to conduct scientific tests to determine the age of the drawings. Why do you think it's important for the experts to reveal the age of the drawings?

NORTHERN MYSTERY

According to the reports, thousands of predynastic rock drawings have been found in the deserts of southern Egypt, but none in northern Egypt, where the cave drawings were discovered.

3. Does this prove the drawings are fake? Why or why not?

NOT IN AGREEMENT

Several Egyptian archaeologists visited the cave site. Some felt the drawings could date back to 7000 B.C. Others believed the art might be from Egypt's Predynastic period.

4. Why do you think the archaeologists have a problem agreeing?

IT MIGHT NOT BE REAL

False means not true or dishonest. Sham refers to trick or fraud, something meant to deceive. Could the Egyptian cave art be an attempt to sham the scientific community?

5. Shade in the letters that spell SHAM and FALSE. Arrange the unshaded letters to spell a prefix scientists use to describe something temporary like the "foot" on an amoeba.

The arranged letters spell __ __ __ __ __ __.

Some say the drawings are fake because no painted rock drawings came from the Predynastic period and the figures and symbols are misshapen.

6. Do you think rock drawings might eventually be found from the Predynastic period? Why or why not?

7. If the drawings prove to be real, what might account for the "poor" art?

BRAIN BUILDERS

Challenge Number One: An archaeologist is a scientist who studies ancient life and culture. Use the letters in ARCHAEOLOGIST to spell the names of eight items scientists may find at an excavation site. You may use a letter more than once.

Challenge Number Two: Rearrange the missing letters in artifact (below) to spell the names of two animals.

__ __ __ i f __ __ __ __

The animals are _____ and _____.

17 Early Man Appears

Standard-Based Concept

Scientists use radiation dating (carbon-14 dating) to find the approximate age of an organism. Carbon-14 dating is based on the fact that all living organisms have the same proportion of carbon-14. Radio carbon dating can date accurately to about 40,000 years.

CRUSTAL SURPRISE

The Earth's crust holds a mystery or two. In 1991, the body of a man emerged from a glacier on the Austrian-Italian border. The frozen corpse became known as Iceman. He lived during the Late Neolithic period, some time between 3300 and 3200 B.C. Artifacts found near the body—bow, arrows, and an axe—indicate Iceman was a hunter.

Kennewick Man, a 9,000 year-old ancient skeleton, appeared along the banks of the Columbia River, Kennewick, Washington. Local Indian tribes believe the remains are those of an ancestor.

SKELETON IN QUESTION

Carbon-14 dating revealed Kennewick Man to be approximately 9,000 years old. Scientists conducted DNA testing of the bones. A major problem arose. Five Indian tribes claimed custody of the remains and ordered a stop to the investigation. They didn't want scientists to disturb the bones of their ancestor. The bones are currently locked up in safekeeping while the scientists and Indian leaders continue to argue.

1. Carbon-14 dating revealed Kennewick Man to be approximately 9,000 years old. Do you think scientists should have the right to continue their examination of Kennewick Man? Why or why not?

CARBON COPY

Every organism in its lifetime absorbs carbon-14 isotopes from carbon dioxide in the _____. This process _____ when an organism _____. Carbon-14 _____ and is not _____. Scientists can tell from the _____ carbon-14 the _____ of the organism.

2. Use the words below to complete the paragraph above. Three of the words do not belong in the paragraph.

decays   lithosphere   element   stops   dies

remaining   begins   age   replaced   atmosphere

Scientists can learn many things from studying ancient bones.

3. What part of the human skeleton do you think might reveal the feeding habits of a person? Why?

GOOD DOGGIE

You and your dog, Femur, are walking through the woods. Femur stops suddenly, sniffs the ground, and begins to dig a hole in the soil. Femur uncovers the remains of ancient human bones.

4. Use the clues to help you identify ten of the bones.

H _ _ _ _	supports the tongue
_ _ _U _ _	lower leg
_ _M _ _ _ _	upper arm
_ _A _ _ _ _	shoulder blade
_ _N _	forearm
_ _B _ _	shin
_ _O _ _ _ _	vertebra
_ _ _ _N _ _	breastbone
_ _ _E _ _ _	kneecap
S_ _ _ _	cranium

NOTE: If you need help in completing the above item, look through the following list of names. The answers are scattered about. Some of the names are bogus and have nothing to do with bones.

tuni	patella	yano	libma	skull	bronchis	sowep
ulna	setta	tibia	fibula	luboy	gemenol	travert
leturi	sternum	thoracic	humerus	slambri	clavicl	femorer
scapula	dyaleno	hurst	clab	scone	stomerus	hyoid

BRAIN BUILDERS

Challenge Number One: There's a bone hiding in one of the tongue twisters below. Find and circle it.

Sister Sally said Sophia sat sidesaddle serenely Saturday.

Billy "Buster" Bailey boasted building a better boat than Bob O'Neill.

Willy Wilding went wading wildly in wacky wavy water.

Challenge Number Two: In what position would you find DNA in the lower jaw?

18 Keeping the Past Alive

—Standard-Based Concept—

Natural and human-caused hazards present the need for humans to assess potential danger and risk.

PAST REFLECTIONS

An earthquake in A.D. 63 crumpled the buildings in the city. In A.D. 79 Mt. Vesuvius erupted and buried the city under tons of volcanic cinders and ash. What city? Pompeii. Pompeii is an ancient city in Southern Italy. In 1748, archaeologists unearthed numerous artifacts, houses, theaters, and temples. They also discovered murals, frescos, and other works of art among the ruins. Unfortunately, the remains of Pompeii, like other ancient buildings from around the world, are slowly being damaged or destroyed by increasing numbers of tourists. Environmental hazards created by temperature, moisture, pressure, and air have also hastened the destruction of these sites.

POMPEII TODAY

Pompeii is the world's oldest archaeological site. Many of the buildings and walls of the city are exposed to natural elements. The sun and rain help wear away the remaining features of the 2,000-year-old complex.

1. Which combination of letters and numbers—a, b, c, or d—reveal ONE of Pompeii's biggest problems? Decode the letters and numbers of each message. Then circle the letter preceding the message that you believe offers the best description. Write the translations in the spaces under the messages.

   a. two + (mu + ch) + hi + H_2O

   _____

   b. knot + (e + nuf) + (in + tear + rust)

   _____

   c. 2 + (men + e) + (two + wrists)

   _____

   d. (why + l + duh) + bee + sts + (row + ming) + the + (straw + eats)

   _____

2. The following situations are contributing to the deterioration of Pompeii. Use the word clues to help you fill in the empty spaces.

These have overgrown	P __ a __ __ s
People are taking these	__ O u __ __ n __ __ s
Moisture or water	__ __ M a __ e
This pigment's fading fast	P __ i n __
There's a lack of care	__ E __ l __ c __
They come in big groups	__ I __ i __ o r __
Sagging overhead covers	__ e I __ i n __ __

TROUBLE-MAKERS?

Scientists play a vital role in the battle of preservation. Some critics say scientists themselves create problems by continuing to dig up new sites. They believe archaeologists should spend more time preserving existing sites.

3. Some archaeologists prefer to hunt for new sites rather than preserve what they already have. Why do you think they feel this way?

IT'S THE RIGHT THING TO DO

A few countries now require archaeologists to care for the site once they finish digging. If the money runs out or the site becomes a major burden, some archaeologists __ __ __ __ __ __ the site. They do this to preserve the area.

4. Use the letters in ERR and BUY to fill in the spaces above for the answer.

BRAIN BUILDERS

Challenge Number One: Use the letters in NATURAL ELEMENTS to answer the following questions. You may use a letter more than once.

a. Too much of this causes some old buildings to crumble: __ __ __

b. This formation often causes metal to decay: __ __ __ __

c. This frozen water may cause damage to fragile structures: __ __ __ __ __

Challenge Number Two: Reread the paragraph under PAST REFLECTIONS. Use the following items to make an illustration of the condition of Pompeii in A.D. 79 on a separate sheet of paper.

a. volcanic cinders

b. volcanic ash

c. a straight line, about 2 inches or 5 centimeters

Early Human Life on Earth: Challenge Activities

1. Find out more about the fossil remains of Lucy. Write a one-page report from what you learn.

2. Make a list and give examples from the list of factors leading to environmental change.

3. Write a one-page report on how early human hunters may have caused large numbers of mammals to become extinct.

4. Imagine that you discovered the remains of an ancient Indian site on a river bank. List six artifacts you found and how you think the Indians used them.

5. Give several examples comparing the work of an archaeologist with that of a paleontologist.

6. Carbon-14 dating showed Iceman to be approximately 5,300 years old. Research how scientists use carbon-14 to date ancient organisms. Write a brief report describing the process.

7. Large numbers of tourists visit newly discovered archaeological finds. Site authorities believe their ability to protect these ruins may be a losing battle. What recommendations would you make to preserve these historic remains?

Section 3
Getting to Know the Lithosphere

This section provides eleven activities concerning the lithosphere. The lithosphere is the rocky outer shell of the Earth, the rigid blocks that make up the crust and upper mantle.

The exercises in this section examine lithospheric phenomena such as volcanic activity (past and present), earthquakes, glaciers, and cave formations. Two activities review current mapping techniques and the GPS-Satellite Navigation Network.

The puzzle exercises, open-ended questions, and brain builder activities in this section are designed to encourage students to use their creative and critical thinking skills. At the end of this section you will find a list titled Challenge Activities. These may serve as a reward for those students who desire extra credit.

19 Leaving the Lava Behind 1

——Standard-Based Concept——

Thick plates cover the Earth's surface. A force deep within the Earth provides energy to move the plates. Plates move with respect to one another. The movement produces enough heat to melt rock underground.

VOLCANIC RUMBLINGS

Melted rock underground known as magma comes to the surface through openings in the Earth's crust. The openings are called volcanoes. Volcanoes belch out molten lava, ash, gas, and solid materials. Magma becomes lava when it reaches the surface. Some examples of lava rock are obsidian, basalt, pumice, and granite. Volcanic mountains are built from molten lava ejected from the Earth's crust.

There are three basic types of volcanoes: cinder cones, shield volcanoes, and composite cones. Explosive eruptions come from cinder cones. They show a narrow base with steep slopes. Shield volcanoes have a broad base and gentle slopes. Composite cones are intermediate in steepness, between the shield volcanoes and cinder cones. Volcanic mountains may grow to a height of 14,000 feet.

MY-O-MAYON

The Philippines are a group of islands off the southeast coast of Asia. A popular tourist attraction known as Mayon volcano rests north of Legazpi. In 2000, Mayon erupted and chased villagers from their homes.

1. The threat of a major eruption from Mayon didn't keep villagers away from their homes too long. They were determined to stand guard over their homes and animals. If they left their property unprotected _ _ _ _ _ _ _ might steal from them. What were they concerned about? Use the letters in SLOT and ORE to reveal the answer. HINT: Find a word that rhymes with scooters and rooters.

2. Do you think villagers who refuse to leave in spite of the danger are foolish? Why or why not?

MAYON OF OLD

Mayon erupted in 1814 and killed more than 1,200 people. Volcanic mudflows buried an entire town.

3. Why do today's villagers face less danger from a Mayon eruption than early settlers did? Give two reasons to support your answer.

MAYON PUZZLE

4. Use the letter clues to help you complete the puzzle.

M _ _ _	what rocks do under intense heat
A _ _ ious	active volcanoes may cause people to become this
_ _ Y	this fills with dust and smoke from eruption
_ _ O _ _	fills the air during a volcanic blast
_ _ _ N _ _ g	a sign of trouble

BRAIN BUILDERS

Challenge Number One: Where could a cone-shaped volcano hide in MAYON VOLCANO?

Challenge Number Two: Use six letters in VOLCANIC ERUPTIONS to spell the name of a major group of organisms damaged or destroyed by volcanic eruptions. You may use each letter only once.

20 Leaving the Lava Behind 2

——Standard-Based Concept——

Volcanoes are not just destructive. They create new landscapes and alter the face of the Earth.

MUCH TALK ABOUT VOLCANOES

They sleep. They awaken. They spit out lava and pump gases and ash particles into the air. Then they calm down. You never know for sure when a dormant (resting) volcano will wake up, start to tremble, and blow its top.

A volcano not only produces lava flows, but it also ejects ash, stones, and deadly gases. Powerful eruptions can create columns of ash and gas able to climb twelve miles or more. Scientists agree that volcanic eruptions have an effect on the weather.

HAVE YOUR RUNNING SHOES READY

Anybody who lives near an active volcano knows how dangerous life can be. The Philippine villagers living within miles of Mayon volcano (Activity 19) remain on constant alert. In January 2002, Mount Nyiragongo (Kigali, Rwanda) belched out enough lava to kill forty people from the city of Goma.

1. What conditions under the surface cause volcanic eruptions to occur? Place the seven statements in their correct order and you'll know the answer. Write the statements in the spaces below.

   - Liquid rock, known as magma, forms deep within the Earth.
   - Heavy solid rock exists under extreme pressure.
   - As more rock melts, magma rises upward.
   - Hot gases, lava, and rocks blast into the air.
   - As pressure decreases, rock begins to melt under intense heat.
   - The magma, mixed with steam, moves into the crust.
   - The magma and gases explode from the Earth.

   (1) _____

   (2) _____

   (3) _____

   (4) _____

   (5) _____

   (6) _____

   (7) _____

2. The flowing lava from Mount Nyiragongo turned many people into fleeing refugees. The eruptions destroyed about 10,000 homes. Circle the letters that spell the names of five items destroyed by the erupting volcano. NOTE: All items appear backwards. Move from left to right as you circle the words.

f l o w r e s c d e n t s g n i v i d o o f
e g g u r t s r e t a w l i q u i o h s a t p
r e t l e h s r i v c o n t r o l p l e h i d e
c r i s i s n o i t a t i n a s c a l d e r a w
t p e w s a c t i v e a v a l g n i h t o l c

3. People often receive signs from nature that a volcano may soon erupt. Write a "sign" on each of the signs below warning of a possible explosion.

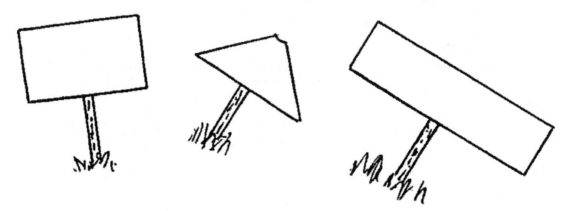

4. Use the letters in SHAG to spell the names of two volcanic products.

Product One: _____   Product Two: _____

VOLCANIC OFFERINGS

5. __ __ __ __ __ __ __ is a dark, fine-grained lava. Water __ __ __ __ __ is an example of a volcanic gas. Unscramble the underlined letters in the names of the volcanoes below and use them to fill in the blanks.

T a m b o r a (Bali area)
M o u n t S a i n t H e l e n s (Washington, USA)
M o u n t V e s u v i u s (Italy)
M o u n t P e l e e (West Indies)
K r a k a t o a (Indonesia)

BRAIN BUILDER

Challenge: Where would you find sodium chloride in basalt, a volcanic rock?

21 Volcano Secrets

——Standard–Based Concept——

Melted rocks rise to the surface, break through the ground, and build volcanic domes. Small fragments of lava and solid rock from volcanic ash spew into the air.

VOLCANO VISIT

In 2000, scientists visited two volcanic regions in Baja California. The first volcano area, San Luis Island, features steep ash cliffs and a huge dome big enough to fill four baseball stadiums. La Reforma, the second stop on the journey, gives hints that a future eruption may occur. Both of these volcanic fields hold a secret or two.

SAN LUIS REVEALED

Scientists believe San Luis volcano erupted within the last 5,000 years. What makes them think so? There seems to be something trapped in the layers of lava rock.

1. Go from left to right and unscramble the four words. Put them together for the answer. Write the answer in the space below.

    l s l e h s   n d a   h e t o r   s o i s l s f

The evidence is present in _____.

CARBON CONTENT

The answer to Number 1 above is the remains of organisms that contained large amounts of carbon while alive on Earth. After death, the carbon decayed into nitrogen at a known rate. The amount of carbon left in the remains reveals the approximate time when the lava buried the organisms.

2. Think of a way to produce an example of salted or smoked meat from carbon.

GRAVITY WINS

During a violent eruption, La Reforma volcano collapsed on its center and formed a crater or caldera. A caldera is a bowl-like cavity produced by intense volcanic action. This occurs when the top half of the cone blows off. Scientists expected the "cave in" to release streams of lava known as pyroclastic flows. Pyroclastic flows consist of rock fragments of volcanic origin. They form rivers of melted lava. To their surprise, no flows could be found. After much investigating, scientists finally located the mysterious hardened remains of the flow on the east side of the volcanic dome.

3. Use your creative thinking ability to describe how the following sketch relates to La Reforma volcano.

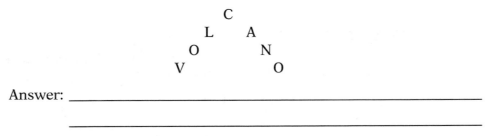

Answer: _____

_____

HEADS UP

4. Use the clues to help you identify signals that may indicate a volcano may soon erupt.

Clues

B __ __ g i __ g	Something happening on the surface of the Earth
__ r O __ __ d	Movement in this material
__ a __ __ O __ dioxide	Gas buildup in the earth
__ t __ __ M	A form of hot liquid

BRAIN BUILDERS

Challenge Number One: ASH needs help. Place a single letter in each space below to complete the term that matches the description.

__ASH	to move quickly
__ASH	skin spots
__ASH	frame holding a glass pane
__ASH	a violent blow
__ASH	money on hand
__ASH	crush or damage

Challenge Number Two: In 1982, El Chicon, a volcano in Mexico, erupted and sent a plume of ash twenty-two miles into the stratosphere. Scientists say the ash traveled about forty-five miles per hour and circled the Earth. How many days did it take the ash to complete the journey? (The Earth's circumference is nearly 25 thousand miles.)

22 Earthquakes 1

——Standard-Based Concept——

Crustal plates move at a slow rate. Plate motions are believed to produce earthquakes, volcanic eruptions, and mountain building.

A NERVOUS PLANET

An earthquake occurs when the Earth's crust moves rapidly. Movement takes place along a fault or crack in the Earth's crust.

1. Find and circle the words in the puzzle that rhyme with the paired words below. The rhymed words describe how the earth may move during an earthquake. Answers may be up, down, forward, backward, and diagonal.

```
T  R  E  M  B  L  E  S
D  S  O  R  S  J  E  E
L  N  E  W  H  T  R  L
X  A  A  F  A  T  O  B
K  Y  I  R  K  S  L  M
S  E  B  G  E  U  L  U
C  I  M  W  S  R  S  R
V  P  A  S  U  C  O  F
```

a. days, maze; b. moles, poles; c. rakes, takes; d. stumbles, crumbles; e. thimbles, symbols

AWAKE TO A QUAKE

Earthquakes rock Japan on a regular basis. Japan is located above four tectonic plates that move across the Earth's surface. In 2000, the island of Miyakejima (near Tokyo) received two major jolts with magnitudes of 6.2 and 5.8. Magnitude refers to the measure of the strength of an earthquake.

2. Large numbers of homes are built on active fault zones. They pop up along the Pacific Coast (USA) like wildflowers in the spring. The Pacific Coast is a well-known area for earthquake activity. Why do you think people choose to live in earthquake-prone areas?

IN THE BEGINNING

As pressure builds in the Earth's crust, things begin to happen. Scientists say pressure buildup triggers the beginning of an earthquake.

3. Use arrows to connect the word and phrases showing how an earthquake may develop.

   a. rocks move   b. energy waves are produced

                      c. pressure

   d. crustal rocks   e. tremors are detected

                      f. rocks break at weak points

MAJOR SHAKE

In January 2001, India suffered a killer earthquake. Rescuers counted over 6,000 dead a few hours after the quake. Almost 100 villages were flattened by the quake. Indian officials estimated damages at $2.17 billion.

4. What was the magnitude of the quake? Solve the following problem for the answer: (a) Divide 0.6 into 10.5; (b) Multiply the answer by 2.6; (c) Add 2.4 to the total; (d) Subtract a pair of 20s from the answer to Item c. The magnitude of the quake was _____. NOTE: This is an arithmetic exercise.

5. Some villagers refused to return to their homes after the quake. Where might they find shelter?

6. What kinds of emergency services do you think the villagers should receive?

BRAIN BUILDERS

Challenge Number One: Where an earthquake begins is called the focus. Why haven't photographers been able to take pictures of this event?

Challenge Number Two: The point on the Earth's surface directly above the focus is known as the epicenter. Where would frozen water be found in the word epicenter?

23 Earthquakes 2

——Standard-Based Concept——

Earthquakes and volcanic eruptions are examples of how changes occur in the ongoing evolution of the Earth's system.

ENERGY WAVES

When crustal rocks break and slide past each other, energy shock waves travel away from the focus. Primary or P waves travel through solid and liquid material, Secondary or S waves travel through solids but not through liquids. When these waves reach the surface, a third type of wave appears. What letter represents the surface wave?

1. Draw a line through the letters in the puzzle that answer the two questions and you'll solve the problem.

   a. What produces up-and-down back-and-forth motion?

   b. What earth material supports plant life?

F	A	U	L	T	C
S	W	B	O	E	R
C	A	F	A	N	U
U	V	I	D	E	S
S	E	R	A	D	P
A	S	O	I	L	E
P	L	A	T	E	S

2. A seismograph is an instrument designed to record earthquake waves. The data appears on a record sheet known as a seismogram. "Seismo" appears in seismograph and seismogram. What do you think "seismo" means?

SHAKY DAYS

A recent federal study listed the metropolitan areas in the United States most likely to suffer from earthquake damage. It gave the cost of destruction in millions of dollars. California cities took fifteen of the top twenty spots on the list. The list included forty cities.

3. Do you think the federal study should concern people living in California? Why or why not?

What's Up in Science?

4. In your opinion, is the federal study important information for those people who live near active fault lines? Why or why not?

5. Arrange the words in the following statement so it will make sense. Then give two examples to support the statement.

Major kill a Human-made people structures earthquake during many.

Example 1: _____

Example 2: _____

BRAIN BUILDERS

Challenge Number One: What does the illustration represent?

Challenge Number Two: What does the illustration represent?

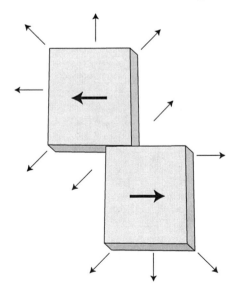

24 Nature's Quake Predictors

——Standard-Based Concept——

Crustal plates seldom rest. They seem to be in constant motion. Plate motions may produce earthquakes, volcanic eruptions, and mountain building.

TREMOR TIME

As early as A.D. 132, the Chinese had an instrument to measure earth vibrations. The funny-looking instrument consisted of dragon heads mounted directly above open-mouthed frog figures. Each dragon head held a ball. Any slight ground movement would cause the ball to fall. If it fell in the frog's mouth, lying directly below, the shock or tremor came from the direction the dragon's head was facing.

1. Use your imagination to design a tremor detector from any of the materials below. RULE: You must use only the listed material. Sketch and label the parts on your model.

   string   empty pop bottle   thread   rubber bands   paper clips
   small jars   funnel   aluminum foil   wire   wooden dowel   tape
   construction paper   modeling clay   small wooden box   scissors
   glue   empty thread spools   small steel bearings

   Place the sketch in the space below.

Tremor Detector

2. Write a brief description of how your tremor detector works.

TAKE A GUESS

No one can be 100 percent sure when an earthquake will happen. Mother Nature makes the decision when and where the quake occurs. However, there are "hints" that an earthquake may soon appear. One clue might be a series of low magnitude tremors known as foreshocks; another is the bulging or lifting of the ground. Instruments designed to measure the buildup of stress in the crust offer a hint of possible danger.

3. Some people have reported strange behavior in animals prior to an earthquake. Unscramble the scattered letters to identify the animals. Then write their names in the empty spaces.

   a. (todners) leave their dens. _____

   b. (skaens) exit their hiding places. _____

   c. (cnksihec) fly into fixed objects. _____

   d. (snaenci) make sharp, abrupt cries. _____

   e. (drsbi) flutter about in the air. _____

NOT SO PREDICTABLE

The owner of Old Faithful Geyser (near Mount Saint Helena, California) predicts earthquakes based on shifts in the geyser's eruption pattern. A scientist studied the patterns and found correlations between the geyser's eruptions and seismic activity within 150 miles.

4. The geyser's eruption patterns aren't effective earthquake warnings because they do not indicate _____ they will happen, _____ they will occur, and the _____ or _____ of an earthquake. Unscramble the group of letters to spell the words needed to complete the statement. Fill in the spaces with the answer. HINT: Some groups of letters will not be used.

   wh   si   pl   gn   it   he   en   ma   whe   at   ze   ace   re   ude

BRAIN BUILDER

Challenge: What do the following series of letters represent? HINT: Think about earthquake motion.

t s r e h m a k o r e s s

25 Glacier Alert 1

——Standard-Based Concept——

Glaciers change the surface of the Earth with their size and weight. They erode the land and carry and deposit material along the way.

ICE MOUNTAIN

A glacier may be described as a huge mountain of slow-moving ice. There are two main types: continental and valley glaciers. Continental glaciers spread across large areas of continents. Continental glaciers cover Antarctica and Greenland. Valley glaciers begin in snowfields at the tops of mountain valleys. They are long, slow-moving streams of ice. Valley glaciers range in length from a few hundred feet to several miles long.

NOT SO FAST

1. If Glacier X moves one inch (2.54 cm) per day, how many days would it take for the glacier to travel the length of a football field (100 yards)?

2. If you were thirteen years old when Glacier X began its journey, how old would you be when it completes the trip?

MELT HAPPENS

A glaciologist is a scientist who studies the development, movements, and general characteristics of glaciers. Glaciologists see a problem occurring in many glacial fields around the world. They say many glaciers are melting at an alarming rate. These melting glaciers are said to be retreating. This seems to indicate a global warming trend.

3. Scientists say Glacier National Park (in Montana) had 150 glaciers over 100 years ago. Today only about 23.2 percent of the original glaciers exist. If so, how many glaciers remain in the park?

What's Up in Science?

MORE MELT

In 2003, a scientific study reported that an Antarctic ice sheet hundreds of miles wide is melting and may be gone in 7,000 years. The melt water could possibly raise global sea levels to 16 feet.

4. Write a response to each of the following statements.

a. "So what? I won't be around in 7,000 years."

b. "People will have plenty of time to adjust to a rising sea level."

c. "Scientists could be wrong. Retreating glaciers have been known to build up their snow fields."

d. "Why worry about it. Humans can't control natural events."

BRAIN BUILDERS

Challenge Number One: If you remove ICE from a GLACIER, what would be left of the glacier?

Challenge Number Two: The first three letters in GLACIER can be rearranged to spell LAG. Lag means "retarded in motion." What four letters in GLACIER can be rearranged to spell a word meaning "to move rapidly"?

26 Glacier Alert 2

——Standard-Based Concept——

Periods of glaciation produce physical and biological changes on Earth. Moving ice can affect an ecosystem.

TOO MUCH WATER

In August 2001, Mount Rainier glacier (in Washington) spilled water into a nearby river, causing it to rise about two feet at the highest point. This proved to be a temporary problem.

1. What do you think caused the release of glacial water? Geologists put the blame on __ __ __ __ __ __ __ __ __ __ __. Unscramble the underlined letters in the question for the answer. Fill in the blank spaces with the missing letters.

2. The excess water caused a debris flow to occur on a local creek and river. Debris means broken bits and pieces of material. Use the letters in the phrase "material in a debris flow" to write the names of four different types of debris. Write their names below. You may use a letter more than once.

    _____, _____, _____, _____

A glacial outburst happens when accumulated water from underneath a glacier pours out. Geologists, scientists who study the Earth, say the excess water did not come from a glacial outburst.

3. List two ways a glacial outburst might pose danger to people living near Mount Rainier glacier.

    a.

    b.

MORE MELTING REPORTS

In July 2002, scientists reported an estimated twenty-four cubic miles of ice melted annually from Alaskan glaciers. They used an airborne laser system to take measurements. Scientific studies suggested the global sea level rose 7.8 inches over the last 100 years.

What's Up in Science?

4. Experts believe the rise in the sea level may be attributed to two things. What do you think they are?

   a.

   b.

5. If glacial melt water gets out of control, lakes can overflow and flood the land. __ o __ e __ t __ and __ g __ i __ u __ t __ r __ could be seriously damaged. Fill in the blanks with the missing letters. CLUE: Here are the scattered missing letters: e c l u s r a f s r

ICE TREASURES

In 2003, a researcher hiking in the Yukon (NW Canada) came across a huge mass of caribou droppings. He found the waste material in an area where there had not been any caribou present for almost 100 years. After a lab analysis, the mystery was solved. The dung had been buried in ice and became exposed when the ice melted. Along with the dung, the scientists discovered darts, arrows, and spears from the Stone Age.

6. Use the hints to help you solve the puzzle listing other items found in the melting glaciers around the world.

   __ __ __ __ __ __   Homo sapiens, people
   __ __ __ __ __ __   cutting tool (rhymes with life)
   __ __ __ __ __ __ __ __   fish, birds, etc. (opposite of plants)

NOTE: Many scientists believe that the burning of fossil fuels is causing an increase in atmospheric carbon dioxide. This, in turn, triggers what is known as the green-house effect. High amounts of carbon dioxide in the atmosphere would trap much of the sun's heat, thus causing the Earth to warm.

BRAIN BUILDERS

Challenge Number One: A dead animal was found in a debris flow. Rearrange four letters in DEBRIS to spell the name of the animal.

Challenge Number Two: Maria told Latisha that "grivaty" gave a glacier its weight. Why did Latisha laugh?

27 Inner Space Travel

——Standard-Based Concept——

Erosion is the removal of material by natural agents—wind, moving water, and gravity. Ground water, an agent of erosion, penetrates into spaces within the rocks of the Earth's crust from caverns.

GROUND WATER IN MOTION

Melted snow and rain sink into the ground and travel through pores and cracks within rocks in the Earth's crust. Some of the water circulates through soluble rocks and dissolves them. Soluble means able to pass into solution. Ground water carries dissolved rocks away in solution.

1. Two examples of soluble rocks are l __ m __ s __ o __ e and d __ l __ m __ t __. Use all of the letters below to fill in the blanks.

   o o i i e e t n

   HINT: The rock names rhyme with rhinestone and dynamite.

2. As ground water dissolves rock and carries it away, the underlying bedrock may become home for ___ ___ ___ ___ ___ ___ ___.

   Unscramble the underlined letters in the sentence and use them to fill in the blanks.

THE MAKING OF A CAVE

As ground water seeps through the pores and cracks in rocks, caves or caverns may develop. Over time, the caverns enlarge into connecting rooms and chambers. Water dripping from above a cavern produces a long spike-like deposit of calcite known as a stalactite. These deposits form on the roof of the cave. The mineral calcite is made of a mixture of calcium, carbon, and oxygen. Calcite deposits form on the floor of the cavern below the dripping water. This formation is called a stalagmite.

3. Make a sketch in the following space of an underground cavern with stalactite and stalagmite deposits.

UNDERGROUND CAVERN

4. Think of a way to help someone remember the difference between a stalactite and a stalagmite. Describe your strategy below.

CAVE VISIT

Caves ranging in size and shape are found throughout the world. New Mexico, Kentucky, and California feature caves in America known for their magnificent formations of stalactites and stalagmites.

The Black Chasm Cavern in Volcano, California, houses a special cave deposit known as helicites. A recent newspaper report (2001) describes helicites as pure calcite growths resembling a mass of electrified pasta. These growths swirl in a bundle of white threads, strings, and twigs. They mesh together like the threads of steel wool.

5. Use the description of helicites to sketch how these structures might appear along cave walls.

6. The public may visit Black Chasm Cavern at certain times during the year. As a visitor, write three statements you believe should apply to the proper conduct of tourists.

   a.

   b.

   c.

BRAIN BUILDER

Challenge: Think of a way to use two letters in changing a small cave into a large cave.

28 Mapping in Outer and Inner Space

——Standard–Based Concept——

Technology is essential to science. It provides instruments and techniques that enable observations of phenomena that are otherwise unobservable due to factors such as quantity, distance, location, size, and speed.

MAP RAP

Maps provide an important tool needed to study the Earth. A television weather reporter without a map would face a tough challenge. Can you imagine an astronomer trying to pinpoint a certain star without a drawing of known points? Earth scientists need maps to examine landforms, pressure and wind patterns, lava flows, crustal movements caused by earthquakes, and so on.

1. You're trying to give somebody directions without knowing any street names or important landmarks. Briefly describe two problems you might encounter.

   a.

   b.

HIGH-TECH MAPPING

In February 2000, the astronauts from NASA's space shuttle Endeavor had completed an awesome task. They used a 197-foot radar mast and antenna to map 43.5 million square miles of the Earth's terrain. The astronauts were able to produce 3-D (three-dimensional) maps of mountain peaks and valleys scattered between Alaska and South America.

2. List two ways you think space mapping would be beneficial to scientists.

   a.

   b.

3. Some people say the government and sponsoring agencies waste too much money on space exploration and related experiments. Do you agree or disagree? Give a reason for your answer.

Mapping in Outer and Inner Space *(continued)*

ONE YEAR LATER

In the summer of 2001, NASA released the 3-D map brought back to Earth by the crew of the Endeavor. Scientists reported the 3-D images of Earth features represent the most accurate global map ever created. The shuttle's radar captured data equal to 160 million pages of text. NASA believes the maps will help aviators, scientists, and the Defense Department. How will these maps assist them?

4. Unscramble the statements below to reveal the answer.

   Aviators: pilots peaks avoid Help mountain into crashing.

   _____

   _____

   Scientists: them patterns valleys Help in study drainage.

   _____

   _____

   Defense Department: with missiles accuracy Department Help Defense guide.

   _____

   _____

UNDERWATER IMAGING

Three-D maps from thousands of feet under the sea produce images of sunken ships and artifacts. High-tech equipment, such as imaging devices and software, produce data taken by a number of underwater sensors.

Modern imaging technology can collect sonar images and other data from the sea floor and compile it into a 3-D digital map of a shipwreck or an airplane crash.

Paul Matthias, the founder and president of Polaris Imaging, has produced thousands of digital images of *Titanic*'s deck. He also created a 3-D map of the *Lusitania*, a British steamship torpedoed by a German submarine on May 15, 1915.

5. Do you think scientists would be interested in using 3-D mapping techniques? Why or why not?

BRAIN BUILDER

Challenge: How could you arrange a map to show the strength of an electric current?

29 Global Positioning System

——Standard–Based Concept——

Technology provides tools for investigations, inquiry, and analysis.

WHAT IS A GLOBAL POSITIONING SYSTEM?

A global positioning system or GPS is a satellite navigation network. This worldwide radio-navigation system uses military satellites. GPS receivers use the satellites as reference points. They can calculate positions anywhere on Earth within a few yards.

1. The military uses GPS to locate certain objects. Find and circle four items in the puzzle of military interest. They may be up, down, forward, backward, or diagonal.

```
E   C   O   N   V   O   Y   S
S   U   M   Q   F   H   R   C
I   B   X   P   A   E   W   A
T   A   J   K   I   D   T   M
A   O   N   D   T   Y   O   I
N   W   L   H   C   Z   G   V
K   O   N   B   R   K   E   L
S   H   E   L   T   E   R   S
```

YOU NEEDED A RECEIVER

A GPS receiver locates satellites and picks up coded radio signals. It translates the time it takes to receive each signal into a distance. The distances combine to pinpoint the location of the receiver. All of the technology works together to fix a position with a high degree of accuracy.

2. Scientists use GPS signals to detect minor earthquake activity. The signals measure ground movements. What two additional natural events do you think you might be interested in monitoring?

   a.

   b.

GPS FOR ALL

In spring 2000, a presidential order encouraged the acceptance of GPS for peaceful, commercial, and scientific use. The public now has access to GPS any time they wish. But before they join in on the fun, users need to purchase a _ _ _ _ _ _ _ _.

3. If you circle the correct answer below, you'll have the letters needed to complete the statement. Then unscramble the letters and place them in the correct spaces.

   a. What name of a cereal grass rhymes with slice?

   oats   wheat   corn   rice   flax

   b. To change direction or course

   exit   veer   shake   jostle   prance

GPS ON VACATION

GPS fits well into the plans of many recreational users. Tech people show a high interest, since GPS can be used in numerous ways. Those who make GPS part of their lives believe it will become a fixture of modern life.

4. Briefly state how GPS might be of value in the following ways:

   a. A person hiking on a trail.

   _____

   _____

   b. A motorist searching for a certain place in a large city.

   _____

   _____

   c. A boat captain heading for a favorite fishing spot.

   _____

   _____

BRAIN BUILDER

Challenge: Figure out a way to get a "signal" from GPS.

Getting to Know the Lithosphere: Challenge Activities

1. Write a one-page report describing active, dormant, and extinct volcanoes. Give an example of each type of these volcanoes.

2. Describe and give examples of six types of volcanic rock.

3. Scientists believe plate tectonics produce earthquakes and volcanic eruptions. Explain with examples how the theory of plate movement may cause these events to happen.

4. Select three famous earthquakes. Describe each earthquake and outline the damage and destruction done by it.

5. Explain how seismologists are able to locate the epicenter of an earthquake.

6. Describe how a tsunami develops when an earthquake occurs. Make a sketch with labels as part of your description.

7. Write a one-page report describing the causes and effects of glacier movement.

8. Describe the beginning, center of accumulation, and the extent of the ice sheets in North America during the last Ice Age.

9. Explain how ground water forms caverns. Name several of the great limestone caves of the United States.

10. Explain how stalactites and stalagmites form in a cave.

11. Do you think the ancient process of cave formation is continuing today? List the geological evidence that would help support your answer.

Section 4

Listening to the Environment

Section 4 presents eight activities with information on chemical poisons in the environment, atmospheric problems created by the greenhouse effect, how global patterns of atmospheric movement influence local weather, and environmental pollution and its effect on living organisms. The concluding activity examines how the loss of the world's wildlife areas may hasten the extinction of certain plants and animals.

The puzzle exercises, open-ended questions, and brain builder activities in this section are designed to encourage students to use their creative and critical thinking skills. At the end of this section you will find a list titled Challenge Activities. These may serve as a reward for those students who desire extra credit.

30 Chromium 6 on Trial

Standard–Based Concept

Natural environments may contain substances (for example, mercury, lead, and Chromium 6) that are harmful to human beings.

THE ELEMENT CHROMIUM

Chromium is a chemical element with a high resistance to corrosion.

24

Cr

52.00

Trace (very small) amounts of chromium are needed in the human body. Chromium gives hardness and strength to other metals such as steel. Chromium makes up to 10 percent of stainless steel. Chromium plays an important role in industry. Its hardness allows it to combine with other metals to form armor plating, metal-cutting tools, and body trim on automobiles.

1. Count the number of times the element symbol for chromium appears in the following paragraph.

    Mr. Crawford's cranberry and crab apple crop ended in disaster. It appears a flock of shiny black creatures called crows cruised creatively over the plants before they landed. Mr. Crawford cried when the creepy critters crumpled his crop.

CHROMIUM 6

Chromium 6, a by-product of chromium, is an odorless, tasteless metallic element. A by-product is anything produced in the course of making another thing.

The water supply to the San Fernando Valley (Southern California) contains Chromium 6 at levels state environmental researchers say are too high.

Scientists believe extensive exposure to Chromium 6 can cause cancer or other serious illnesses. They claim it acts as a cancer-causing agent when inhaled as dust. They are not sure of the damage it causes when ingested.

2. How do you think Chromium 6 found its way into the water supply?

HUGE PROBLEM

3. State and local officials face a big question: water much too chromium is How 6 the much in?

   Unscramble the sentence and write it in the following space:

HOLLYWOOD HYPE

The film *Erin Brockovich* revealed the true story of how Chromium 6 in the soil caused illnesses in a small California town. The amounts of Chromium 6 in the San Fernando Valley are reported to be smaller than those found in the Brockovich film. The smaller amounts arc a big concern for people in the area.

4. Chromium 6 produces two things in the ground water. Use the empty spaces in the puzzle to help you complete the names of the two items. CLUE: One item relates to something toxic; the other refers to pollution. Each word is repeated twice.

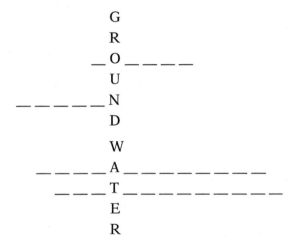

```
        G
        R
    _ O _ _ _ _
        U
_ _ _ _ _ N
        D
        W
_ _ _ _ A _ _ _ _ _ _ _ _
  _ _ _ T _ _ _ _ _ _ _ _
        E
        R
```

BRAIN BUILDERS

Challenge Number One: Think of a way to show Chromium 6 using only one vowel.

Challenge Number Two: Use four letters in CHROMIUM to spell a word meaning a close friend.

31 Mercury Menace

——Standard-Based Concept——

Maintaining environmental health involves establishing or monitoring quality standards related to use of soil, water, and air.

THE ELEMENT MERCURY

The ancient Chinese and Hindus used mercury as early as 1600 B.C. Mercury is the only metal that is liquid at room temperature. Liquid mercury, a heavy metal, may be found in thermometers, vapor lamps, electrical switches, explosives, and poisons.

80

Hg

200.6

MINER PROBLEM

Gold miners during the California Gold Rush used mercury to separate gold from its ore. Records indicate the miners dumped more than 10,000 tons of mercury at different mining sites throughout the Sierra Nevada Mountains.

1. Look at the following illustration. Do you see any evidence of mercury at the mining site? Explain.

Hgasa's Gold Mine

2. Complete the names of four symptoms of mercury poisoning. The groups of letters completing the names are scattered below. There are four extra groups of letters.

oret	para	form	de	lysis
mors	alim	ities	tre	ane
mia	amount	sens		

Match the name of each symptom with the description below.

a. _____ blood disorder
b. _____ shaking or trembling
c. _____ disfigured body parts
d. _____ inability to act or move

MERCURY WITH FINS

Environmental mercury comes from coal-burning power plants and waste incinerators. As mercury accumulates in rivers, bays, and oceans, it becomes absorbed in the bodies of certain fish. Such ocean fish as mako shark, swordfish, striped bass, and tuna are known to be contaminated with mercury. Some freshwater trout, bass, and catfish are "mercury carriers."

3. The Food and Drug Administration (FDA) can restrict the number of commercially caught fish when mercury levels are too high. States may advise the public on how much fish they can safely eat. Do you think people should eat fish known to contain mercury? Give a reason for your answer.

MOTHERS AT RISK

The FDA has warned pregnant women to limit their intake of contaminated fish. Health officials say toxic mercury exposure may produce children with nervous disorders.

4. Kathleen found out she was two months pregnant. She enjoys eating fish at least three times a month. She consumes about twenty-five to thirty pounds of fish a year. Is Kathleen staying within the FDA suggested limit of seven ounces of fish per week? Show your work.

BRAIN BUILDERS

Challenge Number One: Mercury is also known as q __ i __ k s i l v __ __. Use four different letters in MERCURY to fill in the spaces.

Challenge Number Two: Fill in the following blank spaces with words describing three other ways mercury appears.

As a _____, as an _____,

and as a name for a Greek _____.

32 Global Warming Warning 1

——Standard-Based Concept——

Different atmospheric gases become absorbed in the Earth's atmosphere. Absorbed gases act as a greenhouse effect causing the atmospheric temperature to rise.

BLAME THE PLANET

Industrial plants emit gases into the atmosphere. These plants use large amounts of coal and other fossil fuels to operate industrial sites and power plants. Fossil fuels are the remains of ancient plants and animals. These fuels were formed millions of years ago in the Earth's crust.

According to several reports, the increasing production of carbon dioxide and other gases has caused global temperatures to rise. For example, in the northern latitudes temperatures have risen 0.8 degrees Celsius since the 1970s.

1. The burning of certain products releases large amounts of carbon dioxide and other gases into the air. Find and circle three natural products in the puzzle known to produce carbon dioxide. Answers may be up, down, forward, or diagonal.

<pre>
L A R U T A N
S D M R O T S
A N L U L E K
G I S A N D C
W T O A W T S
V C A E L I O
</pre>

TURN ON THE FANS

Scientists agree the Earth is getting warmer. Over time the sun's energy becomes trapped in the lower atmosphere of the Earth. Human production of carbon dioxide and water, plus other natural events, absorb the energy, allowing the atmosphere to increase in temperature.

2. The Department of Energy reported that heat-trapping carbon dioxide emissions increased by ____ percent in the United States in 2000. To find the missing percent, calculate the average for the following numbers:

   3.7   2.8   3.2   3.4   2.4

PROBLEMS ON THE RISE

Many scientists conclude that the continual buildup of heat-trapping chemicals in the atmosphere may cause temperatures to rise several degrees Fahrenheit (anywhere from four to twelve degrees this century). If this happens, future generations may face major problems.

3. Use the number clues near the words below to help you identify three possible problems. Place the missing words in the empty spaces.

> levels 7   caps 5
> 4 ice   1 violent
> 2 storms   polar 3   6 sea

a. An increase in _____

b. A melting of _____

c. Rising _____

THEY CALL IT THE GREENHOUSE EFFECT

A greenhouse is a glass building where the temperature and humidity are controlled for the growth of certain trees and plants. The warm environment helps delicate and out-of-season plants to stay healthy.

Gases emitted from industrial factories are known as greenhouse gases because, like a greenhouse, they tend to warm up the atmosphere. As a result, the absorbed or trapped heat causes an increase in the levels of gases such as carbon dioxide. This event is referred to as the greenhouse effect.

TECHNOLOGY AT WORK

A panel of scientists found plenty of evidence that global warming is a real issue. They believe worldwide release of carbon dioxide and other heat-trapping greenhouse gases are to blame. Where do these scientists find their information?

4. Supply the missing vowels in the following statement to reveal the answer.

Scientists receive information on global warming from c __ m p __ t __ r

c l __ m __ t __   m __ d __ l s and w __ __ t h __ r s __ t __ l l __ t __
d __ t __ .

BRAIN BUILDERS

Challenge Number One: Coal is a black, solid mineral. What would you need to do to change coal into a soft drink?

Challenge Number Two: Tony said to his friend, Graciela: "Did you know carbon comes from one-half of carbon?" What does Tony mean by this?

33 Global Warming Warning 2

——Standard-Based Concept——

Increased atmospheric temperature or global warming may result in climatic changes and rising sea levels.

TREATY TALK

In 1997, several industrial countries came together in Kyoto, Japan, to discuss the global warming problem. They met for the purpose of reducing carbon dioxide and gases emitted into the atmosphere. They formed a treaty. The treaty called for an average 5.2 percent reduction of each nation's 1990 levels of carbon dioxide by 2012.

1. A major world power refused to join the treaty, saying it was unfair and could hurt its country's economic growth. What nation decided NOT to join the treaty? The answer lies hidden in *all of* these five words: SAUSAGE, CAUSAL, LUSATIA (East Germany), MEDUSA, and PUSAN (South Korea). The name of the country is _____.

2. Carbon dioxide is often referred to as _____
_____. Put the scattered letters together in their proper order and you'll have the answer. HINT: The two-word answer rhymes with "mean mouse" and bass (the fish). Place the answer in the empty spaces above.

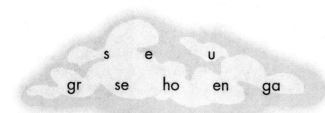

CLIMATE CONCERN

Climate is the average of all weather conditions of an area over a period of years. Recent studies suggest the Earth's climate is warming at an alarming rate. A 2001 study indicates the Earth's temperature could rise by as much as 10.4 degrees over the next 100 years. Scientists refer to this event as global warming.

3. What effect might global warming have on our environment? List six possibilities. Begin each statement with the letter located to the left of the space. The first one is done for you.

C Coastal flooding, carbon dioxide increases, crop failure.

L _____

I _____

M _____

A _____

T _____

E _____

YES, NO, MAYBE

Some people believe human failure to control air pollutants is the major cause of global warming. Others say natural events are to blame. Perhaps it's a combination of factors creating the problem.

4. Write a brief comment about what you think regarding each of the following statements.

  a. Higher temperatures could melt polar ice and raise sea levels by up to ten feet over the next 1,000 years.

  b. Increased temperatures may disrupt the world economy over the next century.

  c. Global warming is caused largely by natural causes.

  d. A steady increase in global temperatures may produce flooding, drought conditions, and other weather shift disasters.

BRAIN BUILDERS

Challenge Number One: Where would you find an example of "fine bits of earth material" in an industrial country?

Challenge Number Two: What four letters in CLIMATE refer to a lack of wind or motion?

34 Ocean Currents and Weather

—Standard-Based Concept—

Global patterns of atmospheric movement influence local weather. Oceans have a major effect on climate because water in the oceans holds a large amount of heat.

El Niño

Ocean currents affect weather patterns. For example, a warm Pacific current known as El Niño appears around Christmas about every three to ten years and lasts around a year. It develops off the coast of South America.

1. The warm tropical waters provide moisture and energy to generate huge "MONSTERS." Actually, instead of MONSTERS, the waters produce _____. Use six letters in MONSTERS to complete the sentence.

2. In the early 1980s, the warm current of El Niño created violent weather conditions. Fill in the missing letters to reveal the impact of El Niño's power in different areas around the world.

   a. r e c _ _ d _ a _ n f _ l _ in C _ l _ f _ r n _ _
   b. _ o _ n a _ o _ s in the _ _ u t _ _ _ a s _
   c. _ l o _ d _ n g in the S _ _ t h _ a _ t
   d. _ l o _ d _ n g in P _ r _ (South American country)
   e. d _ o _ g h _ s in I _ d _ n _ s _ a (Southeast Asia)

SOMEWHERE IN THE MIDDLE

Rising sea surface temperature affects atmospheric pressure. As a result, weather patterns change and produce unexpected weather. Surprisingly, in recent years the tropical Pacific Ocean isn't running unusually hot or cold. It seems to be in a "neutral condition" phase.

3. Why might a "neutral condition" phase pose a problem for scientists?

La Niña occurs when the warm pool of water migrates east. The equatorial Pacific cools as much as eight degrees.

4. Recently La Niña has been blamed for causing "gtuordh from the atrGe Plasin to the uashtSote" in the United States. Unscramble the jumbled words and rewrite the sentence in the empty space.

HINT: the words rhyme with "clout weight pains mouth feast."

GO ARGO

ARGO is an international effort to measure the temperature and salinity of the oceans. The aim of the program is to better understand the impact of oceans on weather and climate around the world. Scientists will use the data to help forecast weather.

In 2000, scientists developed a plan to launch about 3,000 observation buoys to measure the temperature and salinity of the oceans. The buoys, set 180 miles apart, sink to about one mile below the surface. They record the temperature and salinity levels of the layers they pass through. As the buoys surface, they radio their position and send data to a satellite. The cycle is repeated every ten days.

5. Make a sketch in the space below (or on the back of this sheet) to show what this plan looks like. Label ocean surface, buoys, and satellite. Use arrows to indicate how the plan operates.

PELICAN GRIEF

In the Gulf of California the last El Niño event wiped out a large population of pelicans. The warmer than usual currents chased away the favorite food of the pelicans. What is the sea bird's top choice?

6. Solve the following problem for the answer: Replace the "r" in the word that describes what keeps a boat from drifting with a "vy."

The pelican's preferred meal is an _____.

BRAIN BUILDERS

Challenge Number One: What do the eighteen letters below show?

a m t o m i o s s t p u h r e e r e

Challenge Number Two: Salinity refers to the amount of salt in a solution. Where would you find NaCl, sodium chloride, in salinity?

35 Pollution Problem

──Standard-Based Concept──

Causes of environmental pollution and depletion vary from region to region and from country to country. They can accelerate many natural changes.

MAN-MADE MENACE

Pollution occurs when large amounts of industrial chemicals and waste materials enter the atmosphere or waterways. Dust and exhaust fumes from automobiles, businesses, and factories rise into the air and form a hazy blanket known as smog.

1. As cities grow in population, the amount of pollution increases. List two reasons why you think this occurs.

NATURE NEWS

There are times when natural events add to the pollution problem.

2. How might a volcanic eruption create a pollution problem?

3. In what way might a severe earthquake create a pollution problem?

BITS OF PARTICULATES

Very small pieces of matter penetrate the atmosphere. These solid objects mix with gas and liquid materials. They may develop from natural events or appear as a by-product of industrial activities. Scientists refer to these tiny fragments as particulates.

Pollution Problem *(continued)*

4. What do you think makes up particulates? Use the clues to help you complete the puzzle.

		Clues
P __ __ __ __ __		plant grains
A __ __		unburned material
R		
__ __ __ T		black carbon particles
__ I __ __		earth soil
C		
__ U __ __		fine, powdery matter
L		
__ A __ __ __		carbon dioxide, carbon monoxide
T		
__ __ __ __ E		rising vapor from fire
__ __ __ __ S __ __	S P R A Y S	pesticides, cosmetics

5. Particulates may travel hundreds of miles due to m __ v __ __ __ a __ __.
   Use the letters in ORIGIN to fill in the blank spaces.

BRAIN BUILDERS

Challenge Number One: Precipitation refers to the amount of rain or snow. Where would you find rain in precipitation?

Challenge Number Two: Use four letters in CARBON DIOXIDE to spell the name of a gas found in the Earth's atmosphere. One letter may be used twice.

36 Pollution Solution

──Standard-Based Concept──

Human activities can induce hazards through resource acquisition, urban growth, land use decisions, and waste disposal. Such activities can accelerate many natural changes.

UP WITH SOLAR POWER

The sun provides more than enough energy to meet the Earth's power needs. Yet only a fraction of solar energy goes into the power supply. Many areas of the world continue to use such fossil fuels as coal, gas, and oil.

1. Why do you think people continue to rely on fossil fuel for energy?

FROM THE SUN

Scientists use solar cells to convert the energy. Small solar cells provide energy for calculators. Spacecraft rely on solar cells for energy production. Solar cells also provide electrical energy for homes.

2. Solar cells are also known as p_____o_____aic cells. Use the clues to help you complete the sentence. *Clues:* The three-letter word for Part 1 means high temperature, very warm. The four-letter word for Part 2 refers to an electrical unit. The Part 2 word rhymes with the name of a young male horse.

MORE SUN PLEASE

At the present time there isn't enough solar energy available at a reasonable cost to consumers. Energy experts believe the advancement of technology will provide enough solar energy for people in the next few years. Scientists are searching for better ways to capture the sun's energy. Solar energy research is developing smaller, cheaper solar cells.

3. How do you think the increased use of solar powers help the environment?

BAN THE CHIMNEY

In 1993, people living in the San Joaquin Valley (California) were asked to limit the amount of wood burning in their fireplaces. County officials wanted to reduce the buildup of dirty air. Many people ignored the request. In April 2003, the

What's Up in Science?

Pollution Solution *(continued)*

Environmental Protection Agency issued a new rule. The rule banned wood-burning fireplaces in new homes and in subdivisions with more than two houses per acre.

4. Do you think this new rule is fair? Why or why not?

A report stated the San Joaquin Valley has for years failed to meet the federal standard for small particle pollution. Burning wood accounted for a large percentage of the dirty air.

5. Solve the following problem to reveal the percent of air pollution produced by burning wood: Multiply 16.5 by 4.3. Divide the answer by a trio. Subtract 3.65 from the answer. Now add two decades plus 2. Finally, subtract one dozen from the total.

   Burning wood accounts for _____ percent of polluted air.

WHAT'S AN "SSB"?

Maybe some day you'll drive an "SSB" or Super Smog Buster. This would be a non-smog-producing car. In 2003, automakers produced over 100,000 super-clean vehicles. New technology has helped reduce the amount of pollutants entering the air. By 2010, the auto industry predicts there will be three million non-smog-producing vehicles on the road.

6. Do you think cars powered by gasoline could ever become smog-free? Why or why not?

THE BIG H

Automakers are experimenting with fuel cells. Fuel cells use hydrogen and water to make electricity. This technology may eliminate our vehicle exhaust pollution problem.

BRAIN BUILDERS

Challenge Number One: What insect makes up 30 percent of all pollutants?

Challenge Number Two: The burning of gasoline produces a twelve-letter word that can be separated into these words: YARD, HORN, and COBS. What is the twelve-letter word?

37 Forever Organisms

──Standard-Based Concept──

Human activities harm certain living species through population growth, pollution, and overuse and abuse of natural resources.

MAJOR CONCERN

Biologists worry about the loss of natural wealth. Natural wealth includes plants, animals, and the environment. Biologists work hard to develop ways to stop the extinction of plants and animals around the world.

1. What do you think needs to happen before plans to end extinction can occur?

ORGANISMS BEWARE

The behavior of people continues to threaten the existence of certain plants and animals. What are humans doing to damage or destroy these organisms?

2. Eight different problems created by people appear below. Only a part of each problem is revealed. Find the missing parts for each problem and write them in the spaces provided. Note: There are four extra parts included below.

tions	azing	ars	rem	chers
re	ply	son	ution	ttle
ate	ning	ggers	ulation	xic
da	terials	utes		

a. Poa_____ use illegal methods to hunt animals and catch fish. They take over their limit of game.

b. Lo_____ cut down trees for use as lumber. Some people believe too many trees are being cut from the forests.

c. W_____ between na_____ often damage or destroy living organisms and their surroundings.

d. Building of _____ms provide barriers to hold back flowing water. These tend to change the natural environment.

e. Mi_____ serves to remove materials from the earth. This often tears up the surface of the land.

    f. Over ca_____ gr_____ leaves the land void of grass and other vegetation.

    g. Overpop_____ puts a strain on limited sources. Eventually the food and water sup_____ disappear.

    h. Poll_____ poisons the water and air. Many organisms suffer harm from to_____ chemicals and waste ma_____.

WARM TO THE TOUCH

Biologists have identified twenty-five regions throughout the world with vast amounts of plants and animals living within a small area. These regions are known as "hot spots." Scientists believe these hot spots must be protected to prevent extinction. They plan to develop new national parks and wildlife reserves on the hot spots.

3. The figure below reveals how much it will cost to save the hot spots.

<u>$5 billion</u>

next 10 years

Use the information in the figure to answer the following questions:

    a. According to the plan, how much money will be needed over ten years to support each hot spot?

    b. According to the plan, how much money will be needed to support each hot spot per year?

WHERE ARE THE HOT SPOTS?

The rich wildlife areas are spread from continent to continent. Some are located in Asia and Europe; others exist in Central America, Africa, South America, and North America.

4. The names of eight of the Earth's richest hot spots are scrambled below. Unscramble the names and place them in alphabetical order in the spaces under the scattered names.

Bra	Ph	ina	ili	Ca	Co	ran
ngo	lif	nia	ib	Ch	Ca	ean
Ch	iter	ile	Med	zil	ean	or
rr	ppi	nes				

a._____   e._____

b._____   f._____

c._____   g._____

d._____   h._____

Forever Organisms *(continued)*

BRAIN BUILDERS

Challenge Number One: Think of a way to make a sketch showing animals and plants around the world. RULE: You must use only a circle and thirteen letters.

Challenge Number Two: Think of a way to make a sketch of a sign saying "STOP EXTINCTION." RULE: You may use only an eight-sided figure with ten letters.

Section 4

Listening to the Environment: Challenge Activities

1. In November 2003, scientists reported a massive asteroid may have collided with the Earth 251 million years ago and killed 90 percent of all life. Write a report, with illustrations, on how you think such an impact could have affected the Earth's atmosphere.

2. In August 2003, the Bush Administration eased an air-pollution rule on older, coal-burning plants. The operators of these facilities can make equipment upgrades without having to install expensive pollution-control equipment. Write a report defending or criticizing this recent ruling. Give examples to support your argument. NOTE: The plants must still abide by state and federal air pollution laws.

3. Across Northern California (USA) thousands of mines, creeks, and reservoirs are polluted with mercury. Mercury produces a neurotoxin known to be harmful to people and wildlife. Experts cannot agree on what constitutes a "safe level" of mercury. Write a one-page report either supporting or defending this statement: A person should never eat fish known to be contaminated with mercury. Note: For more information, use the following website: www.oehha.ca.gov/fish/hg.

4. Scientists say industrial emissions of carbon dioxide cause climate changes that lead to global warming. Some U.S. government officials and business leaders believe reducing the industrial emissions from carbon fuels would harm the economy. They claim restrictions would lead to shutdowns in manufacturing plants and loss of jobs. Express your feelings about global warming, using examples from newspapers or magazine articles and TV news reports.

5. Research the following question: How does the Environmental Protection Agency (EPA) feel about the Clean Air Act? Provide references from your research.

6. Use information regarding El Niño and La Niña to explain how ocean temperatures affect Earth's climate.

7. Natural changes occur through a variety of human activities. Describe three natural changes that may develop as a result of overpopulation.

8. You have been assigned to protect a "hot spot" (a small area of land with large amounts of plants and animals) from extinction. Describe how you would set up a plan to protect the area from harm.

9. Marine ecology refers to sea organisms and their relationship with their environment. List several ways you think El Niño or La Niña currents affect marine ecology.

Section 5

Ocean Features and Related Creatures

This section includes seventeen activities centering around the ocean environment and various organisms known to live there.

Eight activities highlight such sea animals as coral, shrimp, jellyfish, sea anemone, squid, stingray, sturgeon, and shark. Three activities investigate the sea otter, sea lion, and whale. The remaining exercises address new sea bottom mysteries, pollution concerns, and problems related to animals living around or in the sea.

The puzzle exercises, open-ended questions, and brain builder activities in this section are designed to encourage students to use their creative and critical thinking skills. At the end of this section you will find a list titled Challenge Activities. These may serve as a reward for those students who desire extra credit.

38 Save the Coral

—Standard-Based Concept—

Human activities harm certain living species through population growth, pollution, and overuse and abuse of natural resources.

CORAL NOTES

Corals are tiny animals known as polyps. Polyps have soft bodies and stinging tentacles surrounding their mouths. They resemble sea anemones. Corals reproduce fast, stay close together, and form large colonies. The colonies, along with other species of plants and animals, build coral reefs. Beneath the living colonies lie the skeletons of dead coral. These hard remains support living organisms in the reef community.

1. Use the letters in SPARKLING CORAL REEF HOME to spell the names of six living members of a coral reef community. Refer to the clues to help you complete the puzzle. You may use a letter more than once.

Clues

a. _____   snake-like body; three letters
b. _____   crustacean; four letters
c. _____   seaweed; five letters
d. _____   porous structure; six letters
e. _____   fins and scales; four letters
f. _____   crustacean; six letters

WARM TREAT

Corals prefer to live in a warm, salty environment. Cold, fresh water would wipe them out. They require a water temperature ranging from 70 to 84 degrees Fahrenheit.

2. _ _ _ _ _ _ _ _ _ _ _ _ _ _ _ has caused ocean temperatures to _ _ _ _ _. This is another reason scientists say many coral reefs are facing extinction. Use the scattered letters below to spell the missing words in the sentence above. Note: You will need all of the letters.

i s r g a n r l

b w l e m g i a o

KEEP IT CLEAN

Researchers warn that more than a quarter of the world's coral reefs have been destroyed. They further state that unless major steps are taken, most of the remaining coral could be dead in twenty years. People pollute, and pollution is a major reason coral reefs are dying off.

3. Identify six agents of pollution by filling in the missing letters in the puzzle.

REEF BEEF

In 2000, U.S. President Clinton created an 84-million-acre underwater preserve in the Hawaiian Islands. He did this to help save coral reefs and wildlife.

4. Some people in the Hawaiian fishing industry criticized the plan. They protested because the plan limits fishing and gives the government too much control. Do you agree or disagree with the protesters? Give a reason for your answer.

BRAIN BUILDERS

Challenge Number One: How could you change CORAL into a black, combustible mineral?

Challenge Number Two: How could you make CORAL strong enough to hold a large herd of horses?

39 **Lost City Found**

—Standard–Based Concept—

Features of the ocean floor (magnetic patterns, age, and sea-floor topography) provide evidence of plate tectonics. Hydrothermal vents are a feature of sea-floor topography.

A NICE SURPRISE

In December 2000, ocean scientists reported an interesting discovery. They found a series of pointed, tapering structures resting on a submerged mountain in the North Atlantic. The scientists named these towering spires "Lost City."

The sea floor structures form from hydrothermal vents. The vents, or cracks in the ocean floor, allow warm water from deep in the Earth to flow out. Over time, deposits of minerals from the water build up and form needle-like sculptures known as spires.

1. Sketch a series of spires on the submerged mountain shown below. Make six to eight spires with different diameters.

GOING UP

Scientists toured Lost City in a submersible. A submersible is a vessel built to operate under water. The vessel's crew reported some of the largest spires reached the height of an eighteen-story building and a diameter of thirty feet.

2. Scientists say Lost City extends for about 100 yards (the length of a football field). How many spires of thirty-foot diameter can stand up within an area of 100 square yards?

Lost City Found (continued)

HYDRO HAPPENINGS

Hydrothermal vents appear on the ocean floor at depths of 3,000 feet or more. The hot mineral water may be 600 degrees F or more. You might think nothing could survive in water this hot; yet certain sea organisms live and thrive in a thermal environment.

3. Can you name two sea creatures commonly found near hydrothermal vents? If you need help, refer to the information below. HINT: Looking east to west works the best. You'll have to arrange the letters in proper order.

      Ms. Alc   Data Processor
                         Ocean Research Lab
      Ms. Row   Data Processor Assistant
                         Ocean Research Lab

      Sea Creature #1: _____

      Sea Creature #2: _____

4. How do you think scientists benefit from making discoveries at ocean depths seldom reached by people?

5. What does the statement "The sea holds many secrets" mean?

BRAIN BUILDERS

Challenge Number One: Many hydrothermal vents belch out mineral deposits composed of sulfur and Fe. Circle the chemical symbol for sulfur in MINERAL DEPOSIT. Also, circle the letters that spell the common name for the chemical symbol Fe.

Challenge Number Two: A hydrothermal may be described as a rising column of warm water. The letters that spell heat make up what percent of thermal?

Challenge Number Three: Use all the letters below to write the names of three sea bottom creatures.

      a a b c c l m m o r r w

40 Island Under Water

——Standard-Based Concept——

Technology used to collect data improves accuracy and allows students to analyze and measure results of investigations.

A GOOD SOAKING

A scientist recently discovered an island while examining topographic maps of a sea floor. The island rests under 400 feet of water and stretches over a mile. It lies about twelve miles off the coast of Southern California.

1. What features of an underwater map might indicate the existence of an island?

TALKING IT OVER

Several scientists met to discuss the new find. They believed that near the end of the last Ice Age (16,000 years ago) the island disappeared under the sea. What do you think may have caused this to happen?

2. Rearrange the following words for a possible answer:

    caused   level   sheets   to   Melting
           rise   ice   sea   the

    _____

    _____

3. Could the answer to Item 2 occur within the next sixty years? Why or why not?

4. What could humans do to prevent the answer to Item 2 from occurring?

What's Up in Science?

BEASTS OF LONG AGO

Scientists believe that prehistoric animals may have lived on the island thousands of years ago. They have found fossils of mammal skeletons on nearby islands.

5. Find and circle four mammals known to have lived during the last Ice Age. Write the names next to their descriptions. Answers may be up, down, forward, backward, or diagonal.

S	A	B	E	R	T	O	O	T	H	C	A	T
C	L	A	H	C	L	A	M	K	T	P	S	E
O	L	S	E	A	L	E	D	R	O	E	N	L
R	U	I	F	M	H	L	G	I	M	N	A	G
A	G	F	R	E	C	T	I	L	M	C	K	A
L	U	O	E	L	F	R	B	L	A	T	E	E
B	W	R	A	Y	T	U	N	A	M	O	J	O
H	A	L	I	B	U	T	B	I	R	D	S	T

a. _____humped back, curved horns

b. _____long, curved teeth; cat family

c. _____long neck, humped back

d. _____hairy skin, long tusks

BRAIN BUILDERS

Challenge Number One: See how many spellings of "island" you can get from the following words: iris, landforms, sister, mist, Atlantic, Hawaiian, lily, soldier, dandy, listen, gland, answer. RULE: You may use each letter only once.

Challenge Number Two: Five letters in ISLAND spell the name of a mollusk that lives on land or in the sea. What is it?

41 Don't Go Near the Water

Standard-Based Concept

Maintaining environmental health involves establishing or monitoring quality standards related to use of soil, water, and air.

COASTAL CRUD

There are many different kinds of pollution occurring in the ocean. Much of it exists along the coast, especially closest to shore. Certain pollutants can injure or destroy living organisms within the polluted area. Pollution may upset an environment and change the ecology of an area. Changes may favor some forms of sea life at the expense of others.

A recent study of Southern California beaches showed an 8 percent increase in pollution from 1998 to 1999. Many beaches were closed or posted with health warnings.

1. a. Much of the problem comes from

       __ c __ a __   b __ c __ e __ i __
       1   2   3   4   5   6   7

   Fill in the empty spaces. HINT: The answer sounds like "motion hysteria."

   b. After several trips to the beach, someone might say to you,

      "You __ __ __ really __ __ __."

   Use the letters 1 through 6 from Part (a) to complete the blanks in the sentence for Part (b) HINT: Something about your appearance.

POST THE COAST

Warning postings or closures appear as pollutants reach an unsafe level. A 1996 study in Southern California found that people who swam near a storm drain were 50 percent to 150 percent more likely to report health problems.

2. The postings or closures of California beaches are written in English and Spanish. How do you think people who can't read English or Spanish should be warned of the danger?

Don't Go Near the Water *(continued)*

TOO MUCH OF A WET THING

Pollutants may enter the ocean from rivers, sewer overflows, ocean dumping, and from the air. Many believe runoff (excess water) is the biggest source of ocean pollution.

3. Use the letters in RUNOFF as the first letters for materials that may be found in excess water.

R _____

U _____

N _____

O _____

F _____

F _____

PAIN IN THE DRAIN

Huge populations of people live in cities near the coastline. The settlements need storm protection to carry the excess water to the sea. Large cities like Los Angeles, California, build a network of concrete waterways to prevent flooding. These canals are known as storm drains. The problem comes when urban wastes mix with runoff and pollute the beaches during heavy rain.

As pollution runoff sweeps into the sea, ocean bacterial levels increase. Many of these bacteria cause disease. Runoff mixes with chemical and bacterial agents. Some swimmers report feeling sick and feverish; others complain of upper respiratory ailments.

4. Name four things that you think people might do to help solve the problem of beach pollution.

a.

b.

c.

d.

BRAIN BUILDERS

Challenge Number One: How can the statement "water for fun" be changed into "water runoff"?

Challenge Number Two: How could soil be changed into a chemical pollutant?

42 Fate of the Fish

——Standard–Based Concept——

Human activities harm certain species through population growth, pollution, and overuse and abuse of natural resources.

THINK AGAIN

For years people tossed trash into the ocean. They dumped everything from household garbage to crumpled automobile frames. Humans believed the ocean, with its massive size, would wash away the junk. As rubbish gathered along the coast, it became clear something needed to be done. Now there are laws to prevent dumping debris into the sea.

1. Write a brief response to each of the following statements:

    a. The ocean with its regular tides, strong currents, and pounding waves should be able to handle large amounts of human garbage.

    b. Garbage dumped in the ocean provides food for sea creatures.

FISH STORY

Some fishermen think the ocean will never run out of fish. They believe there's enough water and food to provide a stable environment for years to come. However, recent reports show certain species of fish are declining at a fast rate. New government regulations have placed catch restrictions for certain species. The restrictions also declare some areas off-limits to fishing.

2. Many people believe that we need to "trteopc oru rocseuers." Unscramble the words in quotation marks to complete the sentence.

LEARN THE TERM

The following terms describe the condition of certain species of living organisms:

> AT RISK: to be open to loss or damage.
>
> ENDANGERED: to threaten with extinction.
>
> EXTINCTION: no longer in existence.

3. Circle the term(s) you believe apply to the following statements:

    a. Since the 1960s, the population of some rockfish on the Pacific Coast has declined more than 95 percent.

    at risk   endangered   extinction

Fate of the Fish *(continued)*

b. From 1977 to 1986, fishermen took more than 200 tons of pollock (saltwater fish) near Seattle, Washington. Recent fishing reports failed to find a single survivor.

at risk   endangered   extinction

SWIM FOR YOUR LIFE

Many organisms in the sea appear on threatened or endangered lists. Fishing scientists say that humans can push these creatures toward the brink. The American Fisheries Society listed 82 species of saltwater fish "at risk of extinction."

4. Five of the fish species considered "at risk" appear scattered below. See if you can put them together. Write their complete names in the empty spaces.

ba   pe   ha   s
       but   a   ss
    ch   aw   r
    li   sh   rk

a. ocean _____ (West Coast: five letters)

b. _____fish (Gulf of Mexico: three letters)

c. _____ (Atlantic: seven letters)

d. giant sea_____ (West Coast: four letters)

e. whale_____ (Gulf of Mexico: five letters)

ON GUARD

Atlantic fishermen employ a technique known as longlining to catch swordfish. Longlining allows fishermen to use lines several miles long loaded with hooks. Unfortunately, these lines snag turtles. Some of these turtles are classified as endangered species.

5. What do you think should be done to protect the turtles?

BRAIN BUILDERS

Challenge Number One: What four letters in FISHING combine to give what a fish needs to move?

Challenge Number Two: A boy told his dad that he hooked and lost a twenty-pound salmon. If he lost the fish, how did he know how much it weighed?

Challenge Number Three: Fishermen aren't just men. In fact, you can find two females in every fisherman. How can this be?

43 Microbes from Across the Sea

—Standard-Based Concept—

Some microorganisms—bacteria and viruses—are known to cause certain illnesses.

MICROBE REVIEW

A microbe is a microscopic living thing. It cannot be seen with the naked eye. Bacteria and viruses are examples of microbes. Most bacteria are harmless. However, some of them cause disease in both plants and animals. Microbes that cause human diseases are carried by people, animals, air, water, and food. Viruses carry disease and reproduce only in living cells. Viruses are spread among people by insects, air, water, food, and other people.

1. Use the letters in BACTERIA to spell the names of three mammals and a rodent known to carry bacteria. You may use a letter more than once.

   Mammals: _____, _____, _____

   Rodent: _____

2. Use the letters in ANIMAL AND PLANT VIRUS to spell the names of two mammals, a mollusk, and an insect known to carry virus. You may use a letter more than once.

   Mammals: _____, _____

   Mollusk: _____

   Insect: _____

STAYING IN BALANCE

Health researchers express a concern about ships from foreign countries. They say some vessels bring in harmful bacteria and viruses to U.S. ports. They claim billions of microbes arrive in the ballast water of the ships. Ballast water helps a boat stay in balance or float upright as it sails across the sea.

BALLAST WATER BINGO

In the open sea, the amount of cargo or weather conditions decide when a ship will release its ballast water. In some areas state or federal regulations require a vessel to dump ballast water _____ miles out to sea. Not all ships need to follow the law. In many ports the rule is voluntary. [You'll find the answer in 3(d).]

3. Solve the following problem for the answer in Ballast Water Bingo. Write the answers in the empty spaces.

   a. Add 3½ and 6⅔. Answer: _____

   b. Multiply 12¾ by 8⅘. Answer: _____

   c. Add 50% to the total of (a) and (b). Answer: _____

   d. Subtract Answer (c) from 371. Answer:_____

4. Researchers want tighter restrictions on releasing ballast water near the shore. Why are they pushing for stronger laws?

MICROBES AND FRIENDS

Other organisms join microbes in their journey across the ocean. Researchers say these hitchhiking sea creatures pose a danger to people living near the port areas. Some spread disease-causing bacteria in food; others serve as a general nuisance and need to be removed.

5. The names of three organisms found in the ballast water with the bacteria and viruses are hidden in the series of letters. Circle the letters, put them together, and spell the names of the sea creatures. Write their names in the space provided.

   Row #1:   BAJLELLAYSYT   WFAITSEHR
   Row #2:   BAMLLUASST   WSATEELRS
   Row #3:   BACLLALST   WAATMESR

   Sea Creature #1: _____ HINT: Rhymes with deli dish.
   Sea Creature #2: _____ HINT: Rhymes with hustles.
   Sea Creature #3: _____ HINT: Rhymes with yams.

6. What do you think would be a good way to handle the dangerous ballast water problem?

BRAIN BUILDERS

Challenge Number One: What does a microorganism have in name only?

Challenge Number Two: Which came first—the cafeteria or bacteria?

44 Cormorants Under Siege

——Standard-Based Concept——

An organism's behavior evolves through adaptation to its environment. All animals, including humans, are consumers. A consumer obtains food by eating other organisms.

MEET THE CORMORANT

Cormorants are slender birds with hooked beaks. They have long, flexible necks and stiff tails. Cormorants live along the seacoasts in temperate and tropical regions of the world. Fish is their favorite food.

1. Four fish known to be eaten by the cormorant appear below. Fill in the blanks with the missing letters. Use all of the letters in FAT, SHORT, LOAN, and AS to complete the task.

   C _ _ _ I _ _   T_ _ U _

   S _ _ M _ _   B _ S _

BYE, BYE BIRDIE

Several years ago the double-breasted cormorant population began to decline. Pesticides, water pollution, and armed fishermen killed many birds. The double-breasted cormorant population has rebounded in the last thirty years. The overall increase is about 6 percent annually.

2. Give two reasons why you think the bird population has recovered.

   a.

   b.

TOO MANY CORMORANTS

Cormorants have a large appetite and prefer fish as their favorite meal. This presents a problem. Sport anglers and fish farmers say the large numbers of birds are wiping out the fish.

3. Wildlife officials say an adult cormorant can eat one pound of fish a day. Problem: Lake Mendez holds 12,500 pounds of trout. Approximately how long would it take 72 adult cormorants to eat all of the fish? Assume each adult eats one pound of fish a day.

   Answer:_____

4. In a real-life situation the answer to Item 3 would depend on several factors. List three of the factors. HINT: What things might cause a population of fish to die?

   a.

   b.

   c.

PASS THE BLAME

Some people believe humans created the cormorant overpopulation problem. They say stocked lakes and fish farming attracts large numbers of birds.

5. If you raised fish for a profit (fish farmer), should you be allowed to shoot birds preying on your fish? Why or why not?

TAKING ADVANTAGE

Some fishermen in Europe and Asia use cormorants to catch fish. These birds like to dive deep and chase the fish. Specially trained cormorants catch fish and bring them back to their trainers. Other fishermen tie a string or cord line around the bird's leg. After the bird grabs a fish, the fisherman pulls in the line and takes the fish from the bird.

6. What do you think keeps the bird from eating the fish? The fisherman places something around the cormorant's neck so it won't swallow the fish. The answer appears more than once in the following conversation. HINT: Look for a word within a word.

   Mark: "What did you ask me to do?"

   Carla: "Bring some string with you, Mark."

   Fishermen tie a _____ around the cormorant's neck.

BRAIN BUILDERS

Challenge Number One: Use thirteen letters to show what happens when a cormorant meets a fish.

Challenge Number Two: What is the following illustration trying to say?

Cormorant
Population

45 The No-Wimp Shrimp

──Standard-Based Concept──

An organism's behavior evolves through adaptation to its environment.

SIMPLY SHRIMP

A shrimp may be described as a small, slender crustacean with jointed appendages. Shrimp live in salt- and freshwater. They feed on tiny animals and plants. Other members of the crustacean group include crabs, lobsters, crayfish, and barnacles.

MEAN, MEAN MANTIS MACHINE

A mantis shrimp resembles a praying mantis. This predator, like a praying mantis, carries a strong pair of front appendages. It uses the appendages to grab, hold, and crush its prey.

Mantis shrimp burrow in sand and are mostly active at night. They move at a swift pace. The larger ones (10 cm or more) can pinch human fingers with their claws.

1. The paired words below rhyme with the names of four favorite food items of the mantis shrimp. Write the name of the food item in the space to the right of the paired words.

    a. flab, jab   _____

    b. blimp, limp   _____

    c. pail, tale   _____

    d. dish, wish   _____

SHRIMP ALERT

In 2001, a report from the Monterey Bay Aquarium (California) caught the eye of many readers. It appears a mantis shrimp is eating bottom-dwelling critters from the Splash Zone, a section reserved for visiting children. Two of the Splash Zone organisms being wiped out by the mantis shrimp appear in Item 1 above. Which two are they?

2. To find out, you must first locate the correct term for each of the following definitions. After writing the terms in the empty spaces, you must then combine the letters from the terms to reveal the answers.

    a. An artificial waterway: _____

    b. Bones in the chest cavity: _____

    The two Splash Zone organisms are a _____ and a

    _____ .

The No-Wimp Shrimp *(continued)*

CLEAN HOUSE

Home aquarium owners may lose fish and bottom-dwelling organisms to invading mantis shrimp. Aquarium suppliers sell shrimp traps to them. They also provide triggerfish, known to feed on mantis shrimp. Unfortunately, triggerfish eat bottom-dwelling critters living in the aquarium.

3. Are shrimp traps and trigger fish solutions to the problem, or do they present additional problems? Explain your answer.

4. What would you do to help solve the mantis shrimp problem?

FINAL WORD

The mantis shrimp will be around for a long time. It plays a significant role in watery environments.

5. Use two words from below to complete the statement describing the success of the mantis shrimp.

small	fall	slow	tiny	fast
spiny	middle	little	soft	tall
last	cast	roll	loft	shiny

If a mantis wasn't _____,

its presence wouldn't _____.

HINT: The two words rhyme.

BRAIN BUILDERS

Challenge Number One: Find a word in SHRIMP that describes a naughty child.

Challenge Number Two: What tiny critter, smaller than a shrimp, appears in mantis shrimp?

46 Jellyfish on the Rocks

Standard-Based Concept

Fossils reveal that the surface of the Earth has changed over time and that many different life forms have existed at different times.

ABOUT A JELLYFISH

Jellyfish belong to the phylum Cnidaria. They have a saclike body cavity and stinging cells on their tentacles. They drift with the ocean current and feed on fish and other prey.

ANCIENT DRIFTERS

Fossilized impressions of jellyfish 510 million years old were discovered a few years ago in a Wisconsin quarry. The quarry, thought to be an ancient lagoon, consisted of horizontal stacks of sandstone rock. The jellyfish lie buried in seven layers of rock in the quarry.

A fossil is preserved evidence of past life. Not all organisms die and become fossils. How could a soft-bodied jellyfish beat the odds and leave an impression on rocks?

1. The conditions that may have allowed the jellyfish to fossilize appear in the letters below. Circle the letters needed to complete the sentences. The uncircled letters combine to reveal the mysterious conditions. Go from left to right.

   Q U I O C K B O U R I E A L

   The body of a jellyfish has N __   B __ N __ S.

   L E F O F T T U N D O Y I S T A U R T B E D

   A jellyfish has S __ __ __   B __ D __   P __ R __ S.

OVERWHELMED

The muscles of a jellyfish are too weak to drift against a strong ocean current. Sometimes waves trap jellyfish and wash them onto the beach.

2. Scientists think a high tide or severe storm drove the "quarry" jellyfish onto the shore. The stranded jellyfish died and soon became buried under

   __ __ __ __.

   Use four letters from the word STRANDED to complete the sentence.

Jellyfish on the Rocks *(continued)*

STORY IN STONE

Paleontologists, scientists who study fossils, learn many things about ancient life. What do you think a scientist might discover from examining the fossilized impressions of a jellyfish?

3. Impressions reveal little or nothing about the organism itself. However, an imprint may show the __ __ __ __ __ and __ __ __ __ of an organism. Use nine of the scattered letters in the sketch to fill in the blanks.

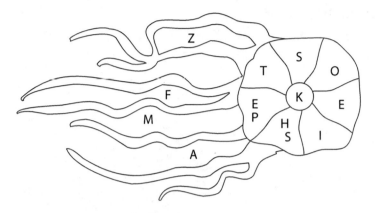

4. Scientists believe the fossil jellyfish resemble modern-day cnidarians. List two observations or conclusions you can make about this statement.

   a.

   b.

BRAIN BUILDERS

Challenge Number One: A jellyfish is an aquatic marine organism. Use eight letters in AQUATIC MARINE ORGANISM to reveal where the jellyfish lives. You may use a letter more than once.

The jellyfish lives in the _____ or _____.

Challenge Number Two: Use the letters in COELENTERATA to spell the names of two different sea organisms. You may use a letter more than once. HINT: The names rhyme with meal and floral. Note: Coelenterata is the old phylum name replaced with Cnidaria.

Challenge Number Three: Use the letters in COELENTERATA to spell the names of two different sea birds. You may use a letter more than once. HINT: The names rhyme with learn and spoon.

47 Anemone by the Sea

——Standard-Based Concept——

Behavior is one kind of response an organism can make to an internal or environmental stimulus. Behavioral response is a set of actions determined in part by heredity and in part from experience.

ANEMONE ZONE

The sea anemone, like its jellyfish cousin, belongs in the phylum Cnidaria. Numerous tentacles surrounding the anemone's mouth give it a flower-like appearance.

Anemones live in rocky areas along the shoreline. They attach themselves to rocks and other solid structures. Some move freely at a slow pace along the sea bottom. Anemones feed on mollusks (snails, clams), crustaceans (shrimps, crabs), and small fish.

1. In the summer of 2003, Disney/Pixar Production came out with an animated underwater film. The sea anemone carries the name of the film. What is it?

   The film title is *Finding* _____.

DUELING TENTACLES

Marine biologists report that anemones stake out and protect their territory. These organisms tend to fight each other to maintain a balance of power within their environment. Anemones use stinging weapons in combat.

2. Anemones fight with tentacles containing poison cells known as

   __ __ __ __ __ __ __ __ __ __ __
   5   6   30 37 42 48 51 66 10 13 26

Anemone by the Sea *(continued)*

Fill in the blanks with the following numbered letters from the indicated sentences in the paragraph above. For example, moving from left to right, the Number 5 letter would be an N, Number 6 letter an E, and so on.

First sentence: 5, 6, 30, 37, 42, 48, 51, 66

Second sentence: 10, 13, 26

IT'S IN THE GENES

Sea anemones are simple organisms with no eyes, no brain, and no language. They protect their territory and fight off other anemones that enter their neighborhoods. Anemones tend not to battle their "relatives."

3. How do anemones know friend from foe? Some scientists believe genetically identical anemones can tell each other apart. They think anemones carry this information in a network of __ __ __ __ __ __ __ __ __ __.

Use the underlined letters in the following sentence to fill in the blanks. The two-word answer rhymes with "serve spells."

Te_n_tacl_e_s of a s_e_a anemon_e_ dis_pl_ay a _va_rie_t_y of _c_olor_s_.

ANEMONE PUZZLER

4. Use the clues to help you complete the sea anemone puzzle.

	Clues
s __ A __ fish	Enemy of the anemone; rhymes with far, car
__ __ N __ __ c __ __ s	Long, slender growth; feelers
__ i __ E pools	Living area; environment
__ M __ __ l fish	Part of anemone's diet
__ O __ y shape	Long and round; rhymes with gaudy
__ N	The "number" in anemone
__ n __ E __ t __ b __ a __ __	Means no backbone

BRAIN BUILDERS

Challenge Number One: Write the word anemone backwards. Now add three letters to the name to change it into a highly remarkable organism. HINT: The first three letters together sound like "fee."

Challenge Number Two: Scientists say simple creatures like the sea anemone have developed a balance of power between expanding territory and keeping it. Show an example of a balance of power using the following word and symbols:

Power   _____   ▲

48 Squid Freak from Down Deep

—Standard–Based Concept—

Scientific investigation sometimes results in new ideas, fresh discoveries, and phenomena to study. Technology used to gather data adds strength and accuracy to scientific discoveries.

SQUID REVIEW

The squid, a member of the class Cephalopoda, carries a thin, streamlined body wherever it swims. The creature resembles an octopus. A squid has good eyesight and can swim rapidly forward or backward. Eight arms and two tentacles help the squid move around and gather food.

NEW VIEW

Since 1989, submersibles videotaped a new species of squid in several ocean basins around the world. These creatures were filmed at depths between 6,000 feet and 15,000 feet.

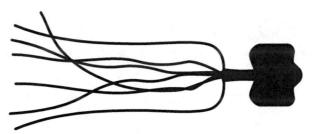

1. How many miles beneath the surface would this be? Anywhere between _____ and _____ miles. Write the numbers in the empty spaces.

2. Why do you think these animals weren't discovered twenty, thirty, or forty years ago? Finish the sentence. Scientists didn't have _____
_____.

3. Fill in the words needed to describe the new organism. The words in parentheses rhyme with the answers.

   a. Its body resembles a (vat) _____ with outstretched (rings) _____.

   b. A cucumber-shaped appendage extends from the (lace) _____ of the body.

   c. The (teacher's) _____ (harms) _____ and tentacles appear long and (win) _____. They seem to sprout from the south (friend) _____ of the appendage.

Squid Freak from Down Deep *(continued)*

　　d.　The arms and tentacles take a (rent) _____-stance position.

　　e.　The arms and tentacles make up about (weighty) _____ percent of the animal's length.

4.　What is the length of a new find? It may reach a length of _____ feet. Unscramble the letters below to reveal a number. Subtract the number from 46 and place the answer in the empty space.

"wtyent rehte"

5.　Here's a question for you, kid: What's inside the BOLDFACED squid?

S c a Q l a U m I a r i D

Circle the letter of the correct answer.

　　a.　Something the squid ate for dinner.

　　b.　A town in southern Italy.

　　c.　A famous Italian opera singer.

　　d.　The squid cooked as food.

BRAIN BUILDERS

Challenge Number One: What do you think the illustration shows?

fish
↕
sea mammals → squid ← birds

Challenge Number Two: Squid produce a substance that they use to help them escape from their predators. The letters needed to spell the name of the substance are found in the words KING, KNIGHT, and KNIT. What is the substance?

49 Stingless Stingrays

——Standard-Based Concept——

Behavior is one kind of response an organism can make to an internal or environmental stimulus.

ALL ABOUT A STINGRAY

A stingray is a flat-shaped fish with wing-like fins. It carries a long, whip-shaped tail.

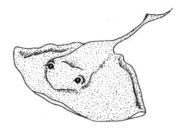

A sharp spine at the base of the stingray's tail allows it to inflict severe stings on people who step on it. The stingray is a close relative of the shark. It feeds on shellfish, squid, and fish.

1. A stingray's stinger or sharp spine goes by another name. Barbara DeBarbetti, fifth-grade student at St. Barbelona Middle School, says the name appears three times in this paragraph. What is it? Thanks for the hint, Barbara. The name is _____.

SOME STAY, OTHERS LEAVE

In 2000, the stingrays at Seal Beach, California, kept swimmers on their toes. The heavy population of stingrays wounded nearly 300 people. Swimmers and waders limped about and grimaced in pain.

2. If you knew danger lurked on Seal Beach, would you stay or go somewhere else? Why?

3. In spite of the danger, some people insisted on staying at the beach. Why do you think they chose to remain?

STINGER NO MORE

Scientists and volunteers got together to try to solve the stingray problem. They used nets to catch large numbers of Seal Beach stingrays. After capturing the fish, they clipped off their stingers.

Stingless Stingrays (continued)

4. Stingrays need their sharp spines to protect them from enemies. Do you think stinger removal would make them vulnerable to predators? Why or why not?

ENEMY ALERT

Scientists say a common enemy of the stingray seldom appears in the Seal Beach area. Therefore, a stingray without a stinger should be safe until the stinger grows back.

5. What is the enemy of the Seal Beach stingray? The two-word answer lies in three words: CASH, OATS, and LARK. Use all of the letters in the three words to reveal the answer. The first word refers to the land next to the sea.

   The enemy is the __ __ __ __ __ __ __ __ __ __ __ __.

PART OF THE PROGRAM

The stingray plays a vital role in the marine food chain. It moves along the sea floor and feeds on bottom-dwelling creatures.

6. What sea organisms would a stingray eat? Use the letters in STINGRAY to help you identify them. The clues will assist you in finding the answers.

   S __ __ __ __   Needed for calamari

   T

   __ __ __ I __ __   Tiny crustacean

   __ __ __ __ __ N __   Fish packed in cans

   G

   __ R __ __   Name rhymes with nab

   __ __ A __   Chowder ingredient

   __ Y __ __ __   A pearl's neighborhood

BRAIN BUILDERS

Challenge Number One: Create a stingray from the following combination of words and letters: gray + s + Sn. HINT: Sn is a chemical symbol.

Challenge Number Two: Here's your chance to play magician. Turn "tiny rags" into a stingray.

50 Plight of the Sturgeon

──Standard-Based Concept──

Human activities can reduce an organism's chance of survival. For example, pollution and overfishing may produce longlasting harm to an environment.

STUFF ABOUT STURGEON

The sturgeon is the world's largest freshwater fish. It has a long, narrow body with bony plates. The fish moves slowly along the river or bay bottom. It eats small animals and plants.

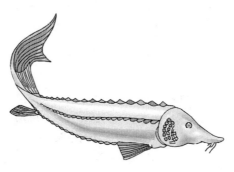

BELUGA: A BIG BRUISER

The beluga sturgeon inhabits the Volga River in Russia. Some grow up to twenty feet in length and weigh more than 3,000 pounds. A few beluga have been known to live more than 100 years. Scientists believe the beluga sturgeon may soon disappear.

1. Why is there a decline in the beluga sturgeon population? Use the clues to help you identify three of the reasons.

   Clues

   a. The result of impure, dirty water. _____
      (nine-letter word)

   b. The act of removing too many fish; exceeding the stock.
      _____ (eleven-letter word)

   c. The act of taking fish in an illegal manner. _____
      (eight-letter word; rhymes with coaching)

WHY? WHY?

Why are people depleting the sturgeon supply? And why do they prefer the female sturgeon over the male? The answer lies in a four-letter word—eggs. The female lays eggs and consumers pay large sums of money to get them. Unscramble the letters in parentheses and fill in the blanks with the answers.

Plight of the Sturgeon *(continued)*

2. A large female beluga sturgeon may lay several hundred _____
   (p n o d s u) of eggs. The eggs are _____ (d e r c u) with _____
   (l a s t), then drained and sealed in _____ (s a c n) or _____ (s a j r).

BIG BUCKS

Some people eat sturgeon eggs. They pay a very high price for these eggs. Sturgeon eggs may sell from $700 to $1,300 a pound.

3. Sturgeon eggs are given a special name. What is it? Unscramble the underlined letters in the paragraph above for the answer. The answer rhymes with star, car, and far.

   Sturgeon eggs prepared for the consumer are known as _____.

STURGEON STEALERS

Poachers, people who break the law, rob the rivers and lakes of female sturgeon. They want the eggs. Eggs bring money, lots of cash. They are not concerned that sturgeon have been fished close to extinction.

4. If sturgeon eggs bring a poacher $900 a pound, how much can a poacher make from 35.5 pounds of eggs?

5. Why do you think poachers continue to break the law?

BRING ON THE BAN

Environmentalists are seeking to ban the import of beluga sturgeon eggs to the United States. They claim a beluga ban will save the beluga sturgeon from extinction. Some experts say a ban will only increase the number of poachers.

6. Do you feel a ban will protect the beluga sturgeon? Why or why not?

7. What do you think should be done to protect the sturgeon?

BRAIN BUILDERS

Challenge Number One: An ore is a mineral with a large amount of metal in it. Think of a way to change ore into fish eggs.

Challenge Number Two: What does this mean? Na fish eggs Cl

51 **Predator Challenge**

——Standard-Based Concept——

An ecosystem consists of all the living and non-living parts of an environment. Predation helps maintain balance in an ecosystem.

PREVAILING PREDATORS

Predators are animals that live by capturing and feeding on other animals.

1. Use the letters in **PREDATOR** to write the names of predators known to live in the ocean. The first one is done for you.

P <u>perch, pelican, porpoise, puffin</u> _____

R _____

E _____

D _____

A _____

T _____

O _____

R _____

2. Use the letters in **PREDATOR** to write the names of predators known to live on land. The first one is done for you.

P <u>parrot, polar bear, panther</u> _____

R _____

E _____

D _____

A _____

T _____

O _____

R _____

PREDATORS ARISE

Reports indicate there have been more predator attacks on humans in North America during the 1990s than ever before. Four predators get the credit for most of the attacks.

Predator Challenge *(continued)*

3. The names of the predators are jumbled together. Write their names in the empty spaces. HINT: Their names sound like elevator, bark, snare, and luger.

c o a l l s h i g b e a r k u g a r a t o r a r

a. _____

b. _____

c. _____

d. _____

STAY ALERT IN FLORIDA

Sharks bit 220 people between 1990 and 2000 in Florida. There were 536 shark attacks worldwide in the 1990s.

4. Name another predator known to attack people in Florida. HINT: The name needs all of the letters in these three words: LOT, AIR, and LAG.

The predator is an _____.

THE FINGER OF GUILT

Wildlife experts say an increase in human population is forcing people to live closer to the animals. Thus, more attacks by predators are likely to occur.

5. Do you think predators harmful to humans should be hunted down and killed? Why or why not?

6. As more people enter the water, there will be more shark attacks. What do you think should be done to reduce the number of shark attacks?

BRAIN BUILDERS

Challenge Number One: Use the letters in PREDATOR to spell the names of a rodent, a female deer, and a large extinct bird. You may use a letter more than once.

Challenge Number Two: Use eight of the letters below to spell predator. What do the remaining letters represent?

P R P E R D E A Y T O R

52 The Sea Otter's Dilemma

——Standard-Based Concept——

Lack of resources and other factors, such as predation, disease, and climate, limit the growth of populations in specific niches in the ecosystem.

KELP FOREST CRITTERS

The sea otter is a marine mammal that lives in the kelp forest. It resembles a weasel. The four limbs of the sea otter are modified for life in the sea. Otters swim using their webbed feet and tail. Sea otters swim, rest, sleep, and eat on their backs. Their bodies are covered with thick fur. Sea otters feed on shrimp, abalone, clams, crabs, and sea urchins.

DISAPPEARING ACT

In 2000, a report stated that sea otters were disappearing from the Aleutian Islands (Alaska). Their population had dropped 70 percent since 1992.

1. Biologists believe a large marine mammal ate many of the sea otters. They say the _____ is to blame. The answer appears backwards in Dacron, a polyester fiber. Write the answer in the empty space.

2. Do you think the sea otter should be moved to a different area for their protection? Why or why not?

COASTAL CONFLICT

Some fishermen make a living by diving for shellfish, such as abalone and sea urchins. Sea otters feast on abalone and sea urchins. A problem arises between fisherman and sea otters.

3. State the problem in a complete sentence.

The Sea Otter's Dilemma *(continued)*

CONTINUING STRUGGLE

In April 2003, forty-five sea otters died along the California coastline. Are fishermen to blame? Not entirely. It seems four things are doing much of the damage.

4. To reveal the causes of the problem, you need to unscramble the words in parentheses. Write the scrambled word in the empty space.

    a. (sartpeia) _____ infections. CLUE: Rhymes with "end in sight."

    b. (btaraice) _____ infections. CLUE: Germs

    c. (bato) _____ injuries. CLUE: Vessel

    d. (hkasr) _____ attacks. CLUE: Hammerhead

The U.S. Fish and Wildlife Service plans to help the sea otter by expanding the mammal's range. The wider range would help protect the population.

5. How do you think this will help the mammal survive?

BRAIN BUILDERS

Challenge Number One: Describe a sea otter with one word having six letters. HINT: Three of the letters are the same.

Challenge Number Two: Use two letters and one number to describe the kind of bed a sea otter prefers.

53 Sea Lions Take Charge

─Standard-Based Concept─

An organism's behavior evolves through adaptation to its environment.

SEA LION NOTES

A sea lion is a marine mammal that lives along the rocky shores. Its streamlined body allows it to glide through the water. The sea lion's forelimbs are modified into flippers. Its main diet consists of fish.

1. Remember the movie *Jaws*? The main character of the film happens to be the sea lion's worst enemy. Name the villain. HINT: The three-word answer needs all of the letters in ARK, WHERE, STAG, and HIT.

   The predator is a _____ _____ _____.

NOT POPULAR IN CALIFORNIA

Saltwater fishermen along the California coast battle with sea lions. Hungry sea lions steal their bait and eat their catch. Fishermen appear to be losing the fight.

A 1972 marine mammal protection act banned hunting sea lions. Since then the California sea lion population has grown from 10,000 to about 200,000.

More sea lions mean increased competition between anglers and the marine mammal for fish.

2. "Sea bombs"—a small explosive—may be used by boat captains to scare sea lions away. They don't work. Why do you think they fail?

Sea Lions Take Charge *(continued)*

3. Some people think it's okay to shoot pesky sea lions. They say the increased sea lion population needs to be "whittled down." What do you think?

DON'T MESS WITH THE MAMMAL

It is illegal to kill or harass any marine mammal unless it poses a direct threat to public safety. Violators face maximum terms of five years in jail and maximum fines of $25,000.

4. How do you think a fisherman who just lost his second salmon to a sea lion might respond to the above statement? (No profanity, please.)

5. Some anglers want Congress to change the Marine Mammal Protection Act so they can kill the harassing sea lions. How do you feel about changing the law?

6. Environmentalists say leave the sea lion alone. Many unhappy anglers believe the mammal should be shot. Use the letters in PEST to describe how an environmentalist and angler might feel about the behavior of a sea lion. The first one is done for you. NOTE: Use nonoffensive words.

Environmentalist	Angler
P proud, puzzled	P put out, pugnacious
E _____	E _____
S _____	S _____
T _____	T _____

7. You don't want to see sea lions harmed. And you think anglers should be able to fish in peace. What do you think Congress should do to help solve the problem?

BRAIN BUILDERS

Challenge Number One: Think of a way to create a seal from a sea lion.

Challenge Number Two: Use five letters in SEA LION to spell the name of a slow-moving animal.

54 A Whale of a Tale

──Standard-Based Concept──

Technology used to gather data adds strength and accuracy to scientific discoveries.

A WORD ABOUT WHALES

The whale is an aquatic mammal. It stays in the water from birth to death. Whales use lungs to breathe air. Some species of whales can hold their breath for more than one hour when diving.

Whales are classified into two distinct groups: The toothed whales and the baleen whales. A baleen whale uses screen-like plates attached to the roof of its mouth to trap food. Toothed whales eat squid and fish. Baleen whales feed on krill (shrimp-like organisms) and plankton (microscopic plants and animals).

Whales may live from 30 to 100 years. Recent findings show some whales may be over 200 years old.

OLDER THAN YOU THINK

A bowhead is a baleen whale. In recent years four bowhead whales killed by Eskimos in Northern Alaska ranged in age from 135 years to 211 years. Scientists used the latest dating technique to determine the age of the whales.

1. Scientists found the age of the bowhead whales by studying changes in _____ acids in the _____ of the whale's _____. Fill in the blanks with three of the words below.
   HINT: See at sea with excellent vision.

lenses	tissue	fins
brain	ears	blood
amino	lacto	eyes
skin	protein	blubber

STUCK IN TIME

Eskimos are members of a group of native North American peoples. They hunt seals, whales, and other sea mammals for food, clothing, and oil.

2. Eskimo hunters have found ancient harpoon points stuck in dead bowhead whales. The harpoon points were made before 1880. How old would one of the whales be if it was killed in 1885?

A Whale of a Tale (continued)

QUIZ TIME

Before we go on, let's find out what you know about whales.

3. Fill in the blanks in the puzzle. Use the three-word clues to help you.

W _ _ _ _   home, habitat, swim

H _ _ _ _ _ _   spear, sharp, barbed

_ A _ _   baby, newborn, young (sounds like half)

_ _ _ _ _ L   vertebrate, mammary glands

_ _ _ _ _ _ E _   under skin, fat (rhymes with rubber)

S _ _ _ _   water, spray, force (rhymes with clout)

HOW ABOUT A DATE?

Scientists can determine the age of a baleen whale by measuring the levels of aspartic acids in the eyes. They have also found the ages of porpoises and other species of whales by using this method.

4. The range of accuracy is about 16 percent in determining the age of a whale. What, then, would be the accuracy range for a whale thought to be 110 years old? How about one believed to be 150 years old?

   a. The range for the 110-year-old would be from ____ to ____ years old.

   b. The range for the 150-year-old would be from ____ to ____ years old.

Some scientists find the age of a whale by measuring the decay of radiation lead samples in bones.

BRAIN BUILDERS

Challenge Number One: Where would you find 2,000 pounds in one tiny plankton?

Challenge Number Two: Baleen whales are the largest whales. What is the difference between a twenty-foot-long toothed whale and a thirty-yard-long baleen whale?

Ocean Features and Related Creatures: Challenge Activities

1. Human activities create problems for certain living organisms. Describe using examples how people abuse natural resources.

2. A United States Coral Task Force was established in 1998. The Task Force wants to preserve 20 percent of coral reefs in U.S. waters as ecological refuges. Write a report on what you believe are necessary steps to protect and preserve an ecological refuge.

3. New undersea discoveries keep scientists alert and excited. Describe at least three modern pieces of equipment needed by scientists to help them with future discoveries.

4. A topographic map shows the surface of an area. Direct measurements of distance and elevation are needed to create topographic maps of land-forms. Only indirect methods work for mapping the sea floor. Write a one-page report describing how research vessels use sonar technology to gain data and study ocean bottom features.

5. According to recent reports, some ocean fish species are declining in population. Many people believe fishermen are largely to blame. Write a two- or three-paragraph response to each of the following statements.
    a. Overfishing is a myth. There are more fish in the ocean today than ever before.
    b. There are too many fishermen and too few fish.
    c. Too many restrictions have driven some commercial fishermen out of business.

6. Research the subphylum Crustacea. Write a report describing at least three members of the group. Include pictures or sketches with your report.

7. The giant squid, Architeuthis, grows to sixty feet in length. It lives at depths of 1,000 to 2,000 feet. Write a report, either pro or con, regarding the following statement: Chances are other large animals live at great depths in the ocean. In time scientists will discover them.

Ocean Features and Related Creatures:
Challenge Activities *(continued)*

8. Many sea otters were discovered sick or dead on the central California coast in April 2004. Researchers found the animals died from parasites in the feces (waste material) of opossums, small marsupial land animals. Write a brief report on how you think the otters came into contact with the feces.

9. Try these math challenges:

   a. In 2000, Russian scientists reported the number of spawning beluga sturgeon had dropped from 26,000 to fewer than 2,000. What is the percent loss of spawning beluga sturgeon?

   b. Sharks bit 220 people between 1990 and 2000 in Florida. There were 536 shark attacks worldwide in the 1990s. What percentage of worldwide shark attacks occurred in Florida during the 1990s?

   c. In 2002, the U.S. Fish and Wildlife Service reported about 3,100 sea otters lived along the California coast. These mammals travel about in search of food. Experts say a sea otter can eat fifteen pounds of food a day. If 80 percent of the 2002 sea otter population ate fifteen pounds of food a day, how many pounds could they eat in a week?

   d. An 800-pound male sea lion can eat up to 8 percent of its body weight in one day. How many pounds of fish can a sea lion eat in a week?

10. Longevity refers to the lifespan of an organism. Whales and humans were thought to have the same longevity. Recent reports show some whales live to more than 100 years old. Write a report stating reasons why you think some whales live so long.

11. The United States government allows Inupiat Eskimos (Northern Alaska) to kill a limited number of bowhead whales each year for food and oil. Write a report giving reasons why you think the U.S. government limits the number of bowhead whales killed.

Copyright © 2004 by John Wiley & Sons, Inc.

Section 6
What's Happening in Space?

Section 6 offers twelve activities featuring celestial objects and mysteries within the universe. Astronomers report new findings in space on a regular basis. This section presents recent data on the discovery of new planets and moons, what scientists learn from studying asteroids, and the surprises brought to Earth by meteorites. Students will become aware of future events planned by space scientists.

The puzzle exercises, open-ended questions, and brain builder activities in Section 6 are designed to encourage students to use their creative and critical thinking skills. At the end of this section you will find a list titled Challenge Activities. These may serve as a reward for those students who desire extra credit.

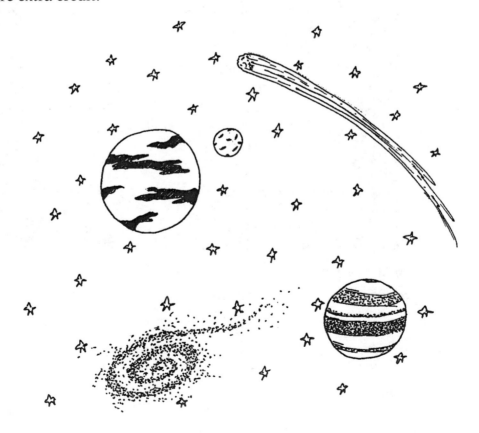

55 Taking on the Universe

——Standard-Based Concept——

Astronomy is the study of the celestial bodies in the universe. Planets, stars, and galaxies are examples of bodies in space. The "Big Bang" theory is the most widely accepted explanation of the formation of the universe.

ON AND ON

The universe is endless space. Planets, stars, and galaxies are spread throughout the universe. There are different ideas about how they got there.

A QUIZ FOR YOU

1. Let's see what you know about objects in the universe. The figure below contains paired items related to space objects. Match the paired items with the space objects by placing the number on the line to the right of the space object.

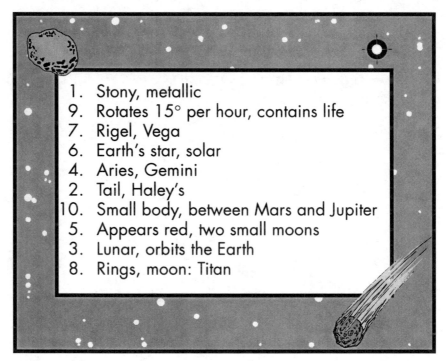

```
 1. Stony, metallic
 9. Rotates 15° per hour, contains life
 7. Rigel, Vega
 6. Earth's star, solar
 4. Aries, Gemini
 2. Tail, Haley's
10. Small body, between Mars and Jupiter
 5. Appears red, two small moons
 3. Lunar, orbits the Earth
 8. Rings, moon: Titan
```

Space Objects

a. stars _____   f. Earth _____
b. moon _____   g. comet _____
c. Sun _____   h. meteor _____
d. Mars _____   i. constellations _____
e. asteroid _____   j. Saturn _____

2. a. How many planets are there in the solar system? Add the numbers for Space Objects b and c. There are _____ planets in the solar system.

   b. Jupiter has at least _____ moons. Add the numbers for Space Objects d, e, and h. Place the answer in the empty space.

   c. Neptune is the ____ planet from the sun. Add the numbers for Space Objects d, g, and h. Place the answer in the empty space.

   d. Saturn has at least _____ moons. Add the numbers for Space Objects i, j, c, and g. Place the answer in the empty space.

   e. Apollo ____ spacecraft photographed the surface of the moon in 1971. Add the numbers for Space Objects e, h, and i. Place the answer in the empty space.

ZIM, BOOM, BANG

The Big Bang theory suggests that the universe began as a massive explosion about 15 billion years ago. The sudden blast spread cosmic material into space. Matter and energy shot out in all directions. The universe began to expand. In time matter began to condense and planets, stars, and galaxies formed. As the universe expanded and cooled, matter formed as we know it today. Galaxies continue to move outward.

3. Studies tracing the galaxies back in time place the Big Bang explosion at 12 billion to 20 billion years ago. Why do you think scientists fail to agree on a specific time when the universe began?

4. Scientists admit they don't have much information about what happened after the Big Bang. Do you think scientists will learn more in future years? Why or why not?

LIGHT FIND

Scientists using high-tech equipment took precise readings of light emitted about 400,000 years after the Big Bang explosion. According to the scientists, these findings will help them understand how the universe has evolved since it began.

5. What question would you like to ask a scientist about this discovery?

BRAIN BUILDERS

Challenge Number One: A planet is a large body that orbits the sun. What three planets in the solar system need three letters from the word PLANET to spell their names?

Challenge Number Two: Think of a way to illustrate an "expanding universe" by using eight letters and five arrows.

56 New Planets in Town

──Standard-Based Concept──

Astronomy is the study of the celestial bodies in the universe. Planets, stars, and galaxies are examples of bodies in space.

PLANET POWER

A planet may be described as a large mass that revolves around a star. Mercury and Venus are the only planets in the solar system without moons. There are nine planets in the solar system.

FAR OUT

Astronomers, scientists who study the sun, moon, planets, stars, and other celestial bodies, have identified over fifty planets beyond our solar system since 1995. Most of these planets appear to be gas giants like Saturn and Jupiter.

1. These planets remain light-years away from Earth. Even our most powerful telescopes cannot detect them. So if we can't see them, why do scientists claim they exist? Unscramble the words in parentheses, place them in the blank spaces, and you'll have the answer.

   A nearby planet causes the home star (star closest to the planet) to _____ (bobewl) due to the force of _____ (vtigary). HINT: The first word rhymes with gobble.

LIGHT, BUT FAST

A light-year is the distance light travels in one year. According to theory, the speed of light—186,000 miles per second—is the fastest possible speed in the universe.

2. The sun is 93 million miles from Earth. How long does it take light to travel from the sun to the Earth?

WHO KNOWS

Astronomers have detected eighteen "planet-like" objects floating in space in the constellation Orion (the hunter). These dark objects are neither planets nor stars.

3. Some planet experts say these are not planets but failed stars known as _____s. Use the clues to help you complete the sentence. (A two-word answer.)

   First Word: A color combining red, yellow, and black.

   Second Word: Stunted growth.

What's Up in Science?

TRAITS OF A PLANET

4. Four surface features that appear on some planets are hidden in the puzzle below. Circle the letters that spell the name of each feature. Answers may be up, down, forward, backward, or diagonal.

X	B	Z	H	G	P
G	J	M	E	L	Y
V	E	Y	A	B	T
C	L	I	F	F	S
Q	N	J	E	W	U
S	K	C	O	R	D

HINT: The answers rhyme with rains, stocks, must, and whiffs.

EVEN MORE PLANETS

In 1998, four astronomers detected a planet about fifteen light-years from the sun. It has more mass than Jupiter and orbits the home star—Gliese 876—every sixty-one days.

5. Why do you think this might be an important find for astronomers?

Gliese 876 is a red dwarf star. Red stars have a surface temperature of less than 3,500 degrees centigrade. A red dwarf is a dim, low-mass star. Scientists say red dwarf stars exist for a longer time than any other stars.

6. Do you think a planet orbiting a red dwarf star might support life if conditions were favorable? Why or why not?

BRAIN BUILDERS

Challenge Number One: Our planet, Earth, is a mighty planet. Use the letters in MIGHTY PLANET to spell the names of two major life groups that live on Earth. You may use a letter more than once.

Challenge Number Two: Some of the letters in LIGHT-YEAR are needed to spell the name of a planet. What are the letters?

57 Mars: A Watery World?

——Standard-Based Concept——

Modern technology allows scientists to make new discoveries in space. Unmanned space probes have sent numerous photos back to Earth from the planet Mars.

PRESENTING MARS

Mars is the fourth planet from the Sun. It shows a reddish color to the naked eye. People refer to Mars as the "red planet." Mars has a thin atmosphere. Deep canyons and volcanic craters cover the surface of Mars. Canyons and grooves in the surface may have been eroded by ancient streams and rivers.

THINK THIRST

Could there be water on Mars? Before you answer, read the following statements about Mars: (1) The atmospheric pressure is too low for water to exist as a liquid. (2) The temperature is too low for water to exist as a liquid. Therefore, liquid water may not be present on Mars. Do you think water might exist in another form?

1. Scientists believe a wet climate once prevailed on Mars. U.S. spacecrafts found evidence of __ __ __ __ __ __ __ by __ __ __ __ __. Use the letters scattered below to help you fill the blanks. HINT: Three letters make a "wet" chemical formula; seven letters combine to describe a "general wearing away."

   r o i o s e H O n H

2. New evidence suggests water may be trapped in two different places on Mars. Write the possible locations in the spaces below.

   One: R A L O P E C I S P A C (three words)

   _____

   Two: S R I O V R E S E R R E D N U E H T E C A F R U S (four words)

   _____

   _____

   HINT: Read in reverse from left to right; then you'll succeed in this twisted plight.

What's Up in Science?

Mars: A Watery World? *(continued)*

HYDROGEN HINTS

Molecular hydrogen measurements give an indication of the amount of water that may once have existed on Mars. Some scientists believe vast oceans once covered Mars. Scientists analyzed data that measured the amount of molecular hydrogen (H_2) in the atmosphere of Mars. The scientists measured the hydrogen in the Martian atmosphere. Researchers believe the data support the theory that ancient Mars may have had enough water for an ocean one mile deep.

3. How many times can you spell hydrogen from the letters needed to form the words in the first three sentences under "Hydrogen Hints"?

   Hydrogen can be spelled _____ times.

LIQUID VOYAGE

4. In February 2002, the NASA orbiting spacecraft Odyssey began a 917-day search for water on Mars. Odyssey's thermal emission system detectors and probes are looking for hidden _____ of _____. Fill in the empty spaces with the missing words. HINT: The first word rhymes with rockets, sockets, and lockets. The second word exploded into a mixture of letters: ew ra t

IF AT FIRST YOU DON'T SUCCEED

5. NASA has experienced past failures sending spacecraft to Mars. These failures have cost millions of dollars. Why do you think the United States government is willing to sponsor ongoing Martian spacecraft probes in search of water at a price tag of around $300 million?

BRAIN BUILDERS

Challenge Number One: Think of a way to produce a description of Mars from these words: RAT, LED, and PEN.

Challenge Number Two: Add the letter "W" to "MARS." Then rearrange the letters to produce a word that means a colony of bees.

Challenge Number Three: Add the letter "C" to "MARS." Then rearrange the letters to produce a word that means to leave in a hurry.

58 Asteroid Probes Coming Up

──Standard-Based Concept──

Astronomy is the study of celestial bodies in the universe. Asteroids are examples of bodies orbiting in space.

ASTEROIDS REVEALED

Asteroids are chucks of rocks smaller than planets. Most of them orbit the sun in a path between Mars and Jupiter. Ceres, the largest asteroid, has a diameter of over 1,000 kilometers (over 609 miles). Most asteroids are less than fifty miles wide.

READY TO PROBE

The National Aeronautics and Space Administration (NASA) plans to send a robotic probe into space in 2006. The probe will explore Vesta and Ceres, the two largest known asteroids. The probe will study the asteroids from orbit. Scientists hope to learn several things from the mission.

1. Three pieces of important information appear in the figure. You'll need to unscramble the words and write them in the empty spaces. HINT: The words rhyme with addition, cape, and rise.

sdolve   spaeh   ptenal   cnomotiopis   omon

zies   kocr   wdin   rosal   rast

The key pieces of asteroid data are _____, _____, and _____.

IT'S JUST A THEORY

Did an asteroid crash into Earth and kill the dinosaurs? The asteroid/Earth collision theory suggests that a large asteroid hit the Earth about 75 million years ago. The collision produced a huge cloud of dust, blocking out the sun for years. This caused the temperature to cool down. The colder climate created a massive die-off of species.

Asteroid Probes Coming Up *(continued)*

2. Unscramble the words to produce the terms needed to complete the asteroid/Earth collision theory. You must use all of the letters for each term.

Asteroid/Earth Collision Theory

_____	_____
store, aid (one word)	heart
_____	_____
code, ill (one word)	rest, pile (one word)
_____	
his, van (one word)	

HINT: The words rhyme with devoid, birth, hide, styles, and banish.

FEWER THAN TEN

There are plenty of things to know about asteroids. But you'll only need to find eight of them to complete the following puzzle.

3. Use the clues to reveal eight things about steroids.

	Clues
p __ A __ __ t __ __ d	another name for asteroid
__ e __ __ S __ o __ e	used to find asteroids
T __ n __	describes a small asteroid
__ E __ t	circle of asteroids
__ R __ i __	elliptical path
__ __ O __ __ __ n __ s	number of asteroids
a __ I __	asteroid rotates on this
D __ a __ e t __ __	side-to-side measurement

4. What clues do you think an asteroid might reveal about its origin?

BRAIN BUILDERS

Challenge Number One: Use thirteen letters to show an asteroid in orbit.

Challenge Number Two: What four letters in ASTEROID combine to spell the name of a celestial object?

59 Eros: Space Mountain Asteroid

Standard-Based Concept

Astronomy is the study of celestial bodies in the universe. Asteroids are examples of bodies orbiting in space.

MORE ABOUT ASTEROIDS

Asteroids may be described as chunks of rock that orbit the sun. These space chunks are smaller than planets and have irregular shapes. They are sometimes called minor planets, moons, planetoids, or satellites. They travel in an elliptical orbit.

ENTER EROS

Astronomers like to study Eros, a space mountain asteroid. Other than the moon, Eros comes closer to the Earth than any other celestial objects of comparable size. Astronomers are able to make accurate measurements of its position in space.

Eros, the first asteroid to be orbited by a manufactured satellite, revealed several interesting features. Here are four of them:

- Its potato- or peanut-shaped body measures 21 by 8 by 8 miles in size.
- It has a large groove gouged out near its middle.
- Photos show a solid, rocky body with large boulders scattered about the surface.
- Many craters dot the surface of the asteroid.

1. Use the information above to help you make a sketch of Eros. Place your drawing in the space below. Label three main features found on Eros.

Eros: Space Mountain Asteroid *(continued)*

WHERE Y'ALL FROM?

2. Scientists first thought the asteroid Eros came from a piece of a larger planet or moon. A more recent analysis revealed Eros may be similar to most _____ rocks, in the _____ _____. The three words needed to fill the blanks are in the letters below.

   HINT: First Answer: Numbers 2, 4, 6, 8, 11, 13, 15, 16, and 18. Second answer rhymes with molar piston.

   s p o r l i a m r   s i y t s i t v e e m

WEIGHT PROBLEM

Density is the amount of mass that takes up a certain volume. The density of an object can be determined by dividing the volume into the mass.

3. Water has a density of one gram per cubic centimeter (1 gm/cm^3). Eros shows a density of 2.4 grams per cubic centimeter. Would Eros sink or float in water? How do you know?

4. Asteroid MC-51 has a density three and one-half times greater than Eros. What is the density of MC-51?

SPACE THOUGHTS

5. If scientists discovered a primitive life form on Eros, do you think life might exist on other celestial objects? Why or why not?

6. If you could explore an extraterrestrial body, what would you hope to find?

BRAIN BUILDERS

Challenge Number One: The letters that spell EROS also spell SORE and ROSE. Find another word using the same letters. HINT: Iron, copper, gold, and silver.

Challenge Number Two: Think of a way to create EROS from ASTEROIDS.

60 Paranoid Rhymes with Asteroid

—Standard-Based Concept—

Astronomy is the study of celestial bodies in the universe. Asteroids are examples of bodies orbiting in space.

COVER UP

A paranoid person believes someone or something intends to do harm. This individual may be convinced danger lurks around every corner. It just isn't safe to go outdoors. The same person may seek shelter from an imaginary asteroid that will smash into Earth some time soon. Happily, scientists say the chances of an asteroid/Earth collision are too small to cause concern.

1. Why do you think some people fear being hit by falling space objects?

ANOTHER CLOSE ENCOUNTER

A recent report about an asteroid heading toward Earth sent chills up the spines of many people. The report claimed the asteroid had a one in five hundred chance of hitting Earth.

2. a. The same report states that Earth's orbit and the asteroid's orbit will meet on a certain date. In the space below, draw two orbital paths touching each other. Place a round dot on each orbit. The dots represent the Earth and the asteroid. Label each dot.

b. What must the asteroid and Earth do before they can crush each other?

SURF'S UP

3. Water covers about three-fourths of the Earth's surface. If an asteroid one mile wide hit near a coastline, what might the collision produce? The answer lies hidden in the wave-like pattern below. HINT: Every THIRD letter TOGETHER makes everything better and wetter.

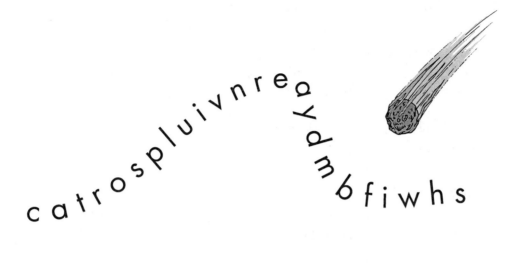

catrospluivnreaydmbfiwhs

4. Many pieces of space material that strike the Earth are never found. Why do you think this is true?

5. Suppose you found a strange-looking rock on the ground. What should you do if you thought the rock came from outer space?

BRAIN BUILDERS

Challenge Number One: Picture a plant with beautiful daisy-like blossoms. Now put together five letters from ASTEROID that will bring the plant to life. HINT: The scrambled letters of the answer spell STARE and RATES.

Challenge Number Two: Think of a way to change an asteroid into a chemical known to produce muscles in athletes.

Challenge Number Three: Use the letters in ASTEROID to spell the name of a rodent, an amphibian, and a female deer. You may use a letter more than once.

61 Twenty-Two and Counting

──Standard-Based Concept──

Astronomy is the study of celestial bodies in the universe. Planets and their moons are examples of bodies orbiting in space.

SATURN SERENE

Saturn is the sixth planet from the sun. The rings encircling Saturn make it unique in our solar system. A spectrograph, an instrument used to study light, shows the rings around Saturn are not solid, but made of rock material mixed with ice. Three other planets—Jupiter, Uranus, and Neptune—also have rings. Saturn has a density less than that of water. Its average temperature is 176 degrees centigrade.

MORE MOONS?

An instrument on a telescope that amplifies light helped detect four new spots of light in orbit around Saturn. Astronomers believe the flecks of light might be moons.

If the scientists are right, then Saturn has a total of twenty-two moons.

1. Many of Saturn's moons are believed to be made up of _____ (6) _____ (5) and _____ (5) _____ (6). Each enclosed letter around Saturn represents a moon. Combine the letters and fill the spaces to complete the statement. HINT: Start at the top of the figure with the letter "F," then move in a counterclockwise direction.

MUCH ABOUT MOONS

2. Many moons of various planets in the solar system show similar features. Find and circle four of them in the following series of letters. HINT: The answers sound like waiters, fountains, galleys, and potatoes.

c i r c u m f e r e n c e v a l l e y s o c e a n s f o r e s t s

b a y s t s u n a m i s s a n d b a r s m o u n t a i n s a l c v

c r a t e r s n o v a s v o l c a n o e s g l a c i e r s t e m o

SIZE WISE

Many scientists work together and check each other's findings. If enough of them agree on something, they will make a news announcement. This held true for the discovery of Saturn's four new moons.

3. Astronomers estimated the new moons are six to thirty miles in diameter. How do they know? They made the prediction based on the a __ __ __ __ t of r __ f l __ __ t __ __ __ i g __ __ from the moons. HINT: The letters needed to fill the blanks are in three words: TUNE, HELD, and COME.

4. What do you think the discovery of new moons reveals about the planet they orbit?

BRAIN BUILDERS

Challenge Number One: Use the letters in SATURN to write the names of two space objects.

Challenge Number Two: STALE and TILE hold the letters needed to spell another name for a moon. What is the other name?

62 The Moons of Jupiter

——Standard-Based Concept——

Astronomy is the study of celestial bodies in the universe. Planets and their moons are examples of bodies orbiting in space.

ENTER EUROPA

Galileo discovered four moons. He found one of them—Europa—orbiting Jupiter in 1610. Almost 400 years later the spacecraft Galileo received information hinting to the possible existence of a salty sea on Europa.

1. Europa has a smooth, bright surface with a coating of ice. The ice might be sixty miles thick. A network of cracks extends along the moon's surface. Based on this information, make a sketch below showing how you think the surface of Europa might appear.

2. Magnetic field measurements taken by the spacecraft Galileo show an electricity-conducting layer beneath Europa's ice cover. Scientists believe this is a strong indication that a salty sea may be present.

   **LIQUID WATER IS CONSIDERED A CRUCIAL
   INGREDIENT FOR LIFE TO EVOLVE.**

   a. If a saltwater ocean exists on Europa, do you think living organisms live there? Why or why not?

   b. If Europa has a sea with living organisms, what do you think they might look like? Use your imagination to help you draw pictures of the organisms in the space below.

The Moons of Jupiter *(continued)*

MEET IO

Jupiter has at least sixteen moons. Io, a Jupiter moon, shakes and rumbles much of the time. Photos from the Galileo spacecraft show the surface of Io dotted with active volcanoes.

3. Measurements indicate the temperature from the flowing lava may reach 3,000 degrees Fahrenheit. The colder areas of the moon show temperatures as low as 280 degrees Fahrenheit. Use the underlined letters to spell the answer to the following question:

    Volcanic activity produced a blanket of yellow material. What substance created the yellow color? Place the answer in the empty space. HINT: It has a rotting egg smell. The element:

    _____.

GREAT GANYMEDE

Ganymede, the largest moon in the solar system, is even larger than the planet Mercury. Scientists believe Ganymede might have a liquid ocean hidden under its frozen surface.

4. Ganymede is the only moon in the solar system known to have its own _____ _____. The scattered groups of letters go together to complete the statement above. The answer sounds like "synthetic yield." Combine the letters and fill the empty spaces. NOTE: There are four extra letters.

    ko tic fi gne eld ma wi

5. Why do you think scientists are interested in finding life on another moon or planet?

BRAIN BUILDERS

Challenge Number One: Europa puzzler: Think of a way to produce ICE WATER from these nine letters:

O H F H N Z R O E

Challenge Number Two: Find and correct the humorous errors in the following statement: Jupiter's moon, Europe, is composed mostly of cork.

Challenge Number Three: Name a state in the United States, a wild animal, and two elements that have the combined letters "io" in their names.

63 Meteor Trails and Comet Tales

——Standard-Based Concept——

Astronomy is the study of celestial bodies in the universe. Meteors and comets are examples of bodies that revolve around the sun.

THE MAJESTIC METEOR

Meteors are small rock or metal pieces that revolve around the sun. The speeding particles "light up" when they reach the Earth's atmosphere. Friction between the fragments and atmosphere cause the meteors to burn up in space. The remains of a meteor fall to Earth as dust.

MIGHTY TINY

Meteors race through the sky each night. If you observe them on a clear night, you might see several streaking across the sky every hour. A meteor the size of a raisin emits brilliant light. How is this possible?

1. _____ _____ (two words) and _____ from the meteor combine to produce a bright flash in the sky. HINT: Fry and heed rhyme with the first two words; feet rhymes with the third word.

2. What do you call a big, bright meteor? It goes by the name _____. Use the letters in FAIR and BELL for the answer. Place the answer in the empty space. HINT: The answer sounds like tire mall.

OODLES OF METEORS

There are times when hundreds of meteors occur in the sky at the same time. These gatherings are called meteor showers. They are named after the constellation (pattern of stars) they seem to come from.

3. In 2001, astronomers made a prediction about the annual arrival of leonids. Leonids are meteors that appear to originate from the constellation Leo. Prediction: Viewers from Earth may see 1,000 or more meteors each hour. If true, how many meteors will be seen every second?

4. What do you think would be the ideal conditions to view a meteor shower?

CONSIDER THE COMET

Science books refer to comets as collections of ice, dust, and gas that orbit the sun. The ice turns into gas and releases the dust in it. A glowing mass becomes the comet's head. The tail of a comet forms as gas is pushed away from the sun. A comet's tail always points away from the sun.

MORE TO TAIL

The sun's rays and the solar wind light up a comet's tail. The tail leaves a beautiful trail in the night sky.

5. Comet X's tail extends 60 million km in space. How many miles would this be? (1 km = 0.621 mile)

FANTASTIC FIND

In 2001, scientists using NASA's Deep Space 1 spacecraft took photos of comet Borrelly. Comet Borrelly shocked the scientists. The photos showed the comet to have a rugged terrain, mountains, smooth plains, and deep fractures.

6. A science book stated the following: "Comets do not contain very much matter." Based on the photos from comet Borrelly, rewrite the science book statement.

BRAIN BUILDERS

Challenge Number One: Produce a comet out of this phrase: "Examples of matter: ice, dust, and gas."

Challenge Number Two: Think of a way to combine a comet and a meteor using eight letters.

64 Meteorite Mysteries

——Standard-Based Concept——

Astronomy is the study of celestial bodies in the universe. Meteors and comets are examples of bodies that revolve around the sun. Meteor fragments that hit the Earth become meteorites.

METEORITE NOTES

Meteorites riddle the Earth's crust. They level forests, punch holes in rooftops, and carve craters in the ground. Meteorites were around long before humans appeared on Earth.

Some scientists believe meteorites are pieces from an unknown planet. According to theory, the mystery planet blew up and scattered fragments into space. Some chunks of material eventually get trapped in the Earth's gravitational field. If a large fragment doesn't burn up in the Earth's atmosphere, it will crash into Earth.

Scientists recognize three main kinds of meteorites: iron-nickel or siderites, stony or aerolites, and siderolites, containing iron and stone material. Iron-nickel meteorites contain about 90 percent iron and about 8 percent nickel. Stony meteorites contain a mixture of oxygen, iron, silicon, and magnesium.

1. Use the information from Meteorite Notes above to help you complete the puzzle.

   _ _ _ _ M _ _ _ _   piece of material

   E _ _ _ _   meteorite's new home

   _ T _ _ _   non-metallic meteorite

   _ _ _ _ E _   meteorite metal

   _ _ _ O _ _   a hypothesis

   _ R _ _   meteorite metal

   _ _ _ _ _ _ I _ _   science expert

   _ _ _ T _ _ _   impact pit or hole

   _ _ E _ _   wide area

WAY BACK WHEN

Scientists estimate the solar system to be about 4.5 billion years old. They say most meteorites are about the same age.

2. Based on this information, do you think meteors and the solar system originated at about the same time? Why or why not?

TAGISH LAKE METEORITE

In January 2000, a meteorite fell on frozen Tagish Lake, located in northern British Columbia. Scientists said the dark fragments contained carbon, nitrogen, and tiny diamonds. Scientists refer to this material as interstellar matter. Interstellar means "among the stars."

3. What does the term "interstellar" indicate about the makeup of a meteorite?

4. Scientists keep the Tagish Lake meteorite in a frozen state. Why do you think they do this?

WHERE'S HOME?

5. Where do meteorites come from? Scientists believe the Tagish Lake meteorite may be a chunk off an _____D. Many _____DS orbit in a belt between Mars and Jupiter. Use two letters from ORBIT, two letters from MARS, and three letters from JUPITER to form the words needed to complete the statement above.

A GOOD QUESTION

The Viking Lander measured the Martian atmosphere in 1976. The atmosphere contained argon, krypton, neon, and xenon.

6. A meteorite studied by scientists contained the same elements as those found on Mars. Does this provide conclusive proof that the meteorite came from Mars? Why or why not?

BRAIN BUILDERS

Challenge Number One: Use four letters in METEOR to spell the name of a woody plant.

Challenge Number Two: Use the letters in INTERSTELLAR PARTICLES to spell the names of three space objects. You may use a letter more than once.

65 From Stars to Galaxies

——Standard-Based Concept——

The origin of the universe remains one of the greatest mysteries in science. The Big Bang theory places the origin between 10 and 20 billion years ago. Stars cluster together to form galaxies. The collection of galaxies in the universe produces most of the visible mass in space.

STAR POWER

Massive nuclear reactions occur on a star. The nuclei of hydrogen atoms fuse (unite) to form helium. This reaction produces heat and light. Our sun, an average-sized star, produces energy in the same way. According to theory, the first stars in the universe appeared 200 million years after the Big Bang.

MIND-BOGGLING

A thousand thousands equal one million or 1,000,000. A thousand millions make one billion or 1,000,000,000. Any way you figure, that's a lot of zeros! Astronomers say there are billions of galaxies in the universe.

1. Using the 0 as the symbol for zero, write in the space below the number of "0's" it takes to make 10 billion. Place the "0's" next to the number 10.

2. Scientists believe the origin of the universe occurred between 10 and 20 billion years ago. The gap of 10 billion years—the number of "0's" from Item 1—raises a question: Why do you think there is a wide range in years?

KEEP GOING

In 2001, astronomers reported finding a mass of quasars and galaxies strung across more than 600 million light-years. A quasar is a star existing far out in space. Quasars send out large amounts of light and radio waves.

The find includes eleven galaxies and eighteen quasars. Together they form a super cluster of celestial objects. How far from Earth is the collection of quasars and galaxies?

3. Astronomers say the cluster is _____ billion light-years away. Solve the following problem and place the answer in the empty blank.

> Multiply 4.5 by 3.2. Divide 2 into the answer.
> Now subtract 0.7 from the last answer.

BLACK HOLES

Scientists describe black holes as massive objects in space. They are thought to form when stars collapse. The collapsing material falls inward and becomes extremely dense. Gravity builds. The gravitational pull becomes so strong that neither light nor matter can escape.

4. Describe a black hole in twelve words or under. Use these terms in your description: collapses, star, dense, gravity, and light.

MILKY WAY MYSTERY

In 1998, astronomers reported they found evidence of a black hole in the Milky Way galaxy. They say it lies in the constellation Sagittarius, 26,000 light-years from Earth.

5. What clues do astronomers use to detect a black hole? They measure the _____ of _____, _____, and dust near the black hole. Astronomers believe stars and celestial matter speed up as the objects come close to a black hole. The broken terms needed to complete the statement are scattered below. Put the terms together and place them in the empty spaces.

| st | ti | ars | |
| on | as | g | mo |

BRAIN BUILDERS

Challenge Number One: Use the letters in INTERNATIONAL ASTRONOMER to write the names of six space objects. You may use a letter more than once.

Challenge Number Two: Find "black hole" hiding in the following sentence: Bob lacks the desire to eat a wholesome meal.

66 Telescopes and Beyond

──Standard-Based Concept──

Technology provides science with the ability to make observations of objects and phenomena in outer space.

TELESCOPE TIME

Telescopes bring distant celestial objects close to Earth. Telescopes use lenses and mirrors to pinpoint objects in the sky. The lenses and mirrors allow an observer to collect light from faraway objects. What do telescopes help astronomers see in space?

1. Use the clues to help you complete the puzzle. ACROSS: 3. Billions of suns. 4. Their tails point away from the sun. 6. Also called planetoids. DOWN: 1. Nine exist in the solar system. 2. Known as "shooting stars." 5. The Earth's partner in space.

X RAY AND AWAY

In 1999, NASA launched the Chandra X-ray telescope into space. X-ray telescopes detect and record X rays emitted from certain space objects. NASA plans to send MAXIM, a more powerful X-ray telescope, into space in 2011.

2. Why do you think NASA wants to send another more powerful telescope into orbit?

3. Chandra costs $1.5 billion. The MAXIM mission will need $800 million to operate. Do you think the government should spend this large amount for another orbiting telescope? Why or why not?

FLYING TELESCOPE

In 2000, NASA reported plans to send a telescope into space by way of aircraft. They call it SOFIA—stratospheric observatory for infrared astronomy. A Boeing 747 jet will carry the telescope into space. The jet, cruising around eight miles above Earth at night, should give astronomers a clear view of the universe.

4. Scientists will cruise at 550 mph with a door open. The open door allows the mirror and mounting of the telescope to be exposed. The temperature will drop to minus 40 degrees. How do you think the scientists will be protected?

"E.T." CALLING

In 2003, astronomers reported plans to place radio telescopes near Lassen National Forest, California. Their objective is to listen for life in space. It will be a full-time search for extraterrestrial intelligence. Sponsors of the plan have provided more than $12 million for the project. The total cost of equipment will reach $25 million.

5. Do you believe life exists in outer space? Why or why not?

BRAIN BUILDERS

Challenge Number One: What three letters in TELESCOPE spell a word that means to observe visually?

Challenge Number Two: Use seven letters in TELESCOPE LENS UNIT to spell the name of a planet.

Section 6

What's Happening in Space?: Challenge Activities

1. Write a report describing the differences between astrology and astronomy.

2. Select a planet in the solar system. List ten true statements about the planet.

3. Write a response to each of the following statements:

   a. Let us suppose water existed on Mars at one time. Why should that concern anyone here on Earth?

   b. Even if Mars had flowing water at one time, it doesn't mean life existed there.

   c. If life did exist on Mars millions of years ago, what do you think it looked like?

4. Scientists make predictions about asteroids crashing into the Earth. Give several reasons why most people pay little attention to these statements.

5. Solve the following arithmetic problems:

   a. An asteroid traveling 68,000 mph recently streaked past the Earth. If the maximum highway speed limit is 65 mph, how much faster than the speed limit is the asteroid going?

   b. A scientist said a person who weighs 200 pounds on Earth would weigh 2 ounces on the asteroid, Eros. Using this information, what would you weigh on Eros? HINT: 16 ounces = one pound; 200 pounds = 3,200 ounces on Earth.

   c. It takes the Earth 365 days or one year to revolve around the sun. If you lived on a planet that took 90 days to orbit its home star (90 days = 1 year), how many days would it take you to age 32.5 years?

6. Some scientists regard comets as carriers of material that made up the early solar system. Reports indicate that some comets orbiting distant stars contain water. Write a statement on what you think this discovery might suggest about other planetary systems.

7. Amino acids form proteins that are necessary for all life. Some amino acids have been found on meteorites. Briefly describe what you think a scientist might do with this information.

8. A meteorite studied by scientists contained the same elements as those found on Mars. This means the meteorite came from Mars. Give several reasons why this statement could be false.

9. If the meteorite in Item 8 actually came from Mars, write an explanation on how you think the meteorite entered the Earth's atmosphere.

10. Scientists say matter near a black hole speeds up before getting pulled into the center of the black hole. Use the above statement as part of a one-half page report on black holes.

11. The Chandra X-ray telescope orbits the Earth. It records X-ray energy from as far away as 12 billion light-years. Find out more about the Chandra X-ray telescope. Write a report on your findings.

12. Radio telescopes are designed to test electronics and software to search for radio signals from space. If extraterrestrials did exist and we could communicate with them, what questions do you think we should ask? List four or five questions.

Life on Land and Water

Section 7 offers ten activities ranging from tiny ants to a bird with a ten-foot wingspan. The exercises feature recent discoveries of worms ten feet or more, crop-destroying crickets, certain amphibians heading for extinction, the return of the California condor, ravaging rodents, and mouse lemurs of Madagascar.

The puzzle exercises, open-ended questions, and brain builder activities in this section are designed to encourage students to use their creative and critical thinking skills. At the end of this section you will find a list titled Challenge Activities. These may serve as a reward for those students who desire extra credit.

67 As the Worm Turns

——Standard-Based Concept——

Biological evolution accounts for the diversity of species developed through gradual processes over generations.

WORM PROFILE

Worms are slender, soft-bodied animals. Some carry a round or flat-shaped body. Segmented worms have ring-like sections or segments. They may live in the soil or prefer fresh- or saltwater habitats. A few worms live as parasites feeding off the body tissues of other organisms.

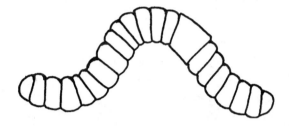

SEA-BOTTOM SENIORS

Scientists have discovered 260-year-old tubeworms living in the Gulf of Mexico. These worms attach themselves to the ocean floor and grow to lengths of ten feet or more. The worms have no eyes or mouth with which to eat. They live in deep water.

1. If they have no mouth to eat with, how do you think they stay alive and continue to grow?

2. How do you think these worms are able to live so long?

HIGH-ALTITUDE WIGGLY

Recently a work crew found a giant earthworm in the higher elevations of the Great Smokey Mountain National Park (East North Carolina and West Tennessee).

3. How long was it? Use the clues in the following message to find the answer.

How many ounces belong in a pound?

How many degrees in a figure round?

Add these together and don't look back,

Now three fifty eight you must subtract.

The giant earthworm was _____ inches long.

NEW SQUIRM TO CONFIRM

An earthworm specialist believes the giant organism is a new species previously unknown to science.

4. What do you think the specialist needs to find out about the earthworm to solve the mystery?

PARASITE PROBLEM

Parasitic worms live on or in the bodies of other organisms. The organisms invaded by parasites are called hosts. Parasites obtain their food from their hosts.

5. *Three-Letter Search:* Four parasitic worms appear below. The name of each worm is missing three letters. Use the worm features to help you fill in the blanks with the missing letters.

Worm Features	*Worm*
a. Flat, ribbon-like body	__ a __ e w __ r m
b. Flatworm trematode	F __ u __ __
c. Roundworm, intestines	A s __ __ r __ s
d. Roundworm, muscular aches	__ r i __ h __ n a

HINT: If you need more clues, search the worm list below. The parasites are hiding among "fake" worms.

Frute	Asboris	Labeworm
Brilhana	Tapeworm	Astirus
Ascaris	Fluke	Gateworm
Trichina	Crilhana	Fruit

BRAIN BUILDERS

Challenge Number One: David <u>u</u>sed a 2-inch worm to catch an 8-inch bass. Then he <u>c</u>aught a 16-inch bass on a 4-inch worm. Finally, his hoo<u>k</u>, baited with a 6-inch w<u>o</u>rm, nailed a 24-inch bass. What wou<u>l</u>d David need to catch a 32-inch bas<u>s</u>? Four of the six underlined letters will give you the answer.

Challenge Number Two: Some worms are classified as roundworms. Where are the two roundest parts of a roundworm?

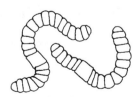

68 It's All About Ants

Standard-Based Concept

All organisms must be able to obtain and use resources, grow, reproduce, and survive in a constantly changing environment.

ANT RANT

Ants seem to appear whenever you run out of insect spray. These six-legged pests may be black, brown, or red. Ants behave in a unique way. They live in colonies with each member carrying out a certain role. They eat other insects, each other, plants, and food scraps.

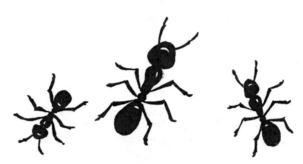

1. Find out something about ants by circling the words in the puzzle that are needed to fill in the blank spaces. Write the circled words in the blank spaces. Answers may be up, down, forward, backward, or diagonal.

B	G	L	A	I	C	O	S	I	T
L	Y	S	A	S	G	U	B	H	Z
E	O	V	P	J	E	A	O	S	S
G	W	H	A	S	X	R	T	E	Y
S	E	E	B	M	A	P	D	Y	N
C	K	A	F	X	L	W	N	E	I
A	B	D	O	M	E	N	H	A	W

   a. Ants belong in the same groups as __ a __ p s and b __ __ s.

   b. Ants live together as a group. They are s __ c __ a __ insects.

   c. Ants have three pair of __ e __ s.

   d. Ants have three main body sections: h __ a __, t __ o __ a __, and an a __ __ o __ en.

NO ANTS, PLEASE

Few animal lovers want ants as pets. Some ants do well in an ant farm. But for the most part, ants are too small, hard to manage, and refuse to learn new tricks.

It's All About Ants *(continued)*

2. Most of all, ants are a __ __ __ __. Use four letters in CARPETS to complete the sentence.

HOT ANTS

In the southern United States the most harmful organism among ants is the fire ant. It carries a powerful sting and can kill livestock and wildlife. The United States government plans to kill fire ants with a phorid fly. Phorid flies released over anthills will inject eggs into the fire ants. After the eggs hatch, the maggots will __ __ __ __ __ __ __ __ __ __ __ the ants by eating the contents of their heads.

3. Use the following clues to find the missing word. (a) Set aside the first four of five from DECAL; (b) remove the "hole" or "cavity" from PITCHER; (c) take three, four, and five from SLATE. Now combine (a), (b), and (c) for the answer. HINT: The answer rhymes with celebrate.

CLASS ACT

A 2000 report described a huge colony of Argentine ants invading California. The colony may extend from Oregon to Mexico. Strangely, the ants seem to get along. Argentine ants usually fight and behave in a rough manner. The Argentine ants in California cooperate and share.

4. How do you think this behavior helps the colony?

ANTS ABROAD

A super colony of Argentine ants has been discovered in Europe. The ant trail extends from Italy to Spain, a distance of 3,600 miles.

5. It appears the ants in Europe are behaving in a similar manner to those in California. Do you think scientists will discover why these ants choose peace over war? Why or why not?

BRAIN BUILDERS

Challenge Number One: Create a way to make an anthill using six ants.

Challenge Number Two: What word would describe a 100-year-old ant? HINT: The word ANT appears in the answer.

Challenge Number Three: What do you call a super-sized ant?

69 Insects Two

—Standard-Based Concept—

All organisms must be able to obtain and use resources, grow, reproduce, and survive in a constantly changing environment.

INSPECT THE INSECT

An insect is an invertebrate. It has no spine or backbone. Chitin—a flexible, hard shell—covers the insect's body. Chitin acts as a protective shield. An insect has three body parts: head, thorax, and abdomen. Most insects have a pair of antennae on the head. Wings and legs grow from the thorax.

INSECT ONE: THE GRASSHOPPER

A grasshopper eats green plants and destroys crops. Whenever grasshoppers go on a feeding frenzy, farmers lose large shares of their profits. Most people can easily identify a grasshopper. Grasshoppers have a pair of wings and short antennae. They also have a large head and big eyes. Their muscular hind legs help them leap from plant to plant.

1. The figure shows a "stripped down" model of a grasshopper. You need to "customize" the insect by adding an eye, antennae, legs, and wings on the sketch. You may wish to refer to a picture of a grasshopper.

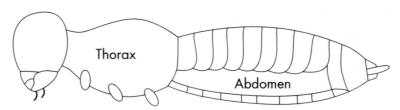

INSECT TWO: CRICKET

Crickets and grasshoppers eat with _____ mouth parts. They share similar features—long antennae and large hind legs. They ruin vegetation, become active at night, and rely on males to emit chirping sounds.

2. Three of the groups of letters below fit together to produce the missing word for the empty space in the paragraph above.

   gri   ip   ch   nd   en   ing   el   wh   ew

3. Why do you think some insects chirp or "sing"?

MORMON CRICKET INVASION

The Mormon cricket is a close relative to the katydid, a member of the grasshopper family. But unlike the katydid, the Mormon cricket devours nearly every plant in its path. The black critters are a mean-eating machine.

In August 2001, the Mormon crickets ate their way through Oak City, Utah. Officials reported more than 1.5 million acres of crops destroyed.

IT HAS HAPPENED BEFORE

Crickets and grasshoppers were no strangers to the early settlers. The Mormon settlers in 1848 lost their crops to hordes of hungry grasshoppers. Huge flocks of a winged animal saved them. These feathered friends swooped in to eat the insects by the thousands.

4. Name the "savior of the fields." Here's a clue: Use the letters in SLUG, plus an extra "L."

   The flying heroes were _____.

BACK TO THE ATTACK

Mormon crickets prefer a quiet, peaceful area in which to reproduce. They seem to choose land owned by the Federal Bureau of Land Management and the U.S. Forest Service. The government put poison in these areas to kill the crickets. In 1999, money for the poisoning program ran out. In 2001, the U.S. government approved a limited poisoning program on Forest Service land. Protests came from environmental groups.

5. Why do you think protesters object to the poisoning program?

6. A single cricket can eat 38 pounds of Farmer Joe's crop in its lifetime. How many tons of food can 1,500 crickets eat before they die? HINT: One ton equals 2,000 pounds.

BRAIN BUILDERS

Challenge Number One: Use six letters in MORMON CRICKET to spell the names of three space objects. You may use a letter more than once.

Challenge Number Two: Use six letters in GRASSHOPPER and CRICKET to write the names of two plant structures these insects destroy. You may use a letter more than once.

70 Where Have All the Froggies Gone? 1

——Standard–Based Concept——

All organisms must be able to obtain and use resources, grow, reproduce, and survive in a constantly changing environment.

APPLAUD THE AMPHIBIAN

Salamanders, toads, and frogs are members of the amphibian group. They are vertebrates, which live both on land and in water. They have _____ skin and provide a food _____ for various vertebrates.

1. Use the letters in MOUSE, SIR, and COT to form the words needed to fill the empty spaces above. The answers rhyme with hoist and horse.

TOAD HITS THE ROAD

A recent report showed a decline in the amphibian population. The study indicated a 15 percent drop rate from 1960 to 1966. The decline in numbers continued at about 2 percent a year through 1997. Scientists say amphibians are physically sensitive to their environment. These creatures "break more easily" than many other critters. Several factors may be causing the decline of amphibians.

2. Unscramble the letters below to reveal five possible reasons for the decline of amphibians. Write the reasons in the empty spaces.

   a. sosl fo nald. _____

   b. ewn dertapsro. CLUE: hunts prey _____

   c. rezilsiterf. CLUE: improves soil _____

   d. citedsepsi. CLUE: kills insects _____

   e. natustlopl. CLUE: causes pollution _____

3. In your opinion, what needs to be done to prevent the amphibian population from falling?

P IS FOR PROTECTION

The Endangered Species Act seeks to protect animals in danger of becoming extinct. The Southwestern Arroyo toad needed help. A large population of Arroyo toads lives in California, between San Diego and Monterey. Land developers were tearing up their habitat. Environmental groups protested.

4. The Fish and Wildlife Service took action. They "of toad aside protection set the for the land." Rearrange the words so the sentence makes sense.

5. Use the letters in AMPHIBIAN to write the three-letter words needed to match the descriptions below. You may use a letter more than once.

Word	*Description*
a. _____	a. metal container
b. _____	b. drawing on a flat surface
c. _____	c. meat from a hog's hind limb
d. _____	d. a place to store food
e. _____	e. to point at a target
f. _____	f. a sudden sound
g. _____	g. front upper part of an apron
h. _____	h. to seize or catch

BRAIN BUILDERS

Challenge Number One: Use five letters to show one-half of a population.

Challenge Number Two: Shanika: "I can prove a two-eyed amphibian can't see." Raul: "Okay, prove it." Shanika gave Raul the proof. What do you think Shanika did?

71 Where Have All the Froggies Gone? 2

──Standard-Based Concept──

Natural systems can change to an extent that exceeds the limits of organisms to adapt naturally.

CRITICAL DECISION

When certain organisms become threatened (in danger of dying out) the U.S. Fish and Wildlife springs into action. The department develops a recovery plan. Many acres of land are designated critical habitat. This allows the plant or animal to be protected from harm.

1. Underline the words in parentheses that complete the following statements:

    a. Organisms (expect, need, insist) protection when they (meet, experience, add) problems in (their, there, they're) environment.

    b. Habitat (protection, prevention, prediction) may cause concern for people who want to (buy, ruin, develop) their land.

    c. A protection plan should (involve, revolve, revive) many (visitors, strangers, people). No private or public organization (welcomes, wants, demands) to be (blamed, honored, forgotten) for wiping out a plant or animal (home, species, cage).

2. If you were responsible for setting up a critical habitat for certain frog species, what kind of environment would you select?

SCATTERED FEATURES

3. There are many body parts that help make up an amphibian. Eight are hiding in the series of letters. Find and circle them. Then place the parts

in alphabetical order in the spaces below the letters. Read the letters from left to right beginning with the first line.

r l s t o n g u e s k p u e y e s a t

i s e b o n e s h e a d o c f l p w

a m b l o o d s k i n b r a t e o s h

o n m u s c l e s t o n e r v e s l k

Alphabetical Order

a. _____   e. _____

b. _____   f. _____

c. _____   g. _____

d. _____   h. _____

4. Use the letters in TOAD as the letters in a word that describes the living area of a toad. Use the clues to help you with the answers.

T _____ CLUE: A plant with branches.

O _____ CLUE: A state in the United States.

A _____ CLUE: A water canal: _____duct.

D _____ CLUE: Earth soil.

BRAIN BUILDERS

Challenge Number One: What does the sketch represent? HINT: The larva of certain amphibians.

```
T
A
D
T
A
D
```

Challenge Number Two: Where would a human appear in a salamander?

Challenge Number Three: Find a toad hiding in the following sentence:

What does a student need to do to advance one grade level?

72 The California Condor Comeback 1

——Standard-Based Concept——

Extinction (or near extinction) of a species occurs when the environment changes and the species fails to adjust to changing conditions.

CONDOR COMMENTS

The California condor is the largest flying bird. An adult bird can reach thirty pounds. Its wingspan extends to nearly ten feet. The population of the California condor fell to nine in 1985. These birds were fewer than ten away from becoming extinct.

MORE CONDOR COMMENTS

The California condor has a naked, brightly colored head. A dark plumage (coat of feathers) covers its body. Condors eat the meat of dead animals. Native Americans included the condor in their religious ceremonies. They believed the condor held supernatural powers.

According to the following data, the California condor nearly reached extinction in 1985.

Year	Number of Birds
1950	150
1985	9
1988	27
1992	63
2000	164
2002	198

1. By what percent did the California condor population drop from 1950 to 1985?

2. By what percent did the California condor population increase from 1988 to 2002?

The answers to Items 1 and 2 bring up two questions: Why did the California condor almost die off? And what caused the bird population to revive?

The California Condor Comeback 1 *(continued)*

ABSURD WORD

A *raptor* is a bird of prey. A vulture eats *carrion*, dead animals. Both words apply to the California condor, since it preys on the carcasses of dead critters.

3. If Mr. Condor received "joy and pleasure" from eating carrion, then you face a challenge. There's a word describing a feeling of joy and pleasure. Vulture and raptor combine to form the word. What is it? Write the letters to the word in the empty spaces. HINT: Three letters from RAPTOR and four letters from VULTURE will produce the answer.

— — — — — — —

4. Identify seven animals that serve as carrion for the California condor. Use the hints to help you find the answers.

	Clues
C __ __ __ __ __	wild animal; dog family
__ A __	a pet with soft fur
R __ __ __ __ __	has soft fur with long ears
R __ __	long-tailed rodent
__ I __ __	feathered creature
O __ __	predatory night bird
__ N __ __ __	limbless reptile

BRAIN BUILDERS

Challenge Number One: Think of a way to show how the word MEAT reveals what a condor eats.

Challenge Number Two: What four letters in CONDOR combine to spell an animal's shortened name?

73 The California Condor Comeback 2

──Standard-Based Concept──

All organisms must be able to obtain and use resources, grow, and reproduce while living in a constantly changing environment.

TOO MANY TOXINS

Toxic refers to poison. If an animal eats lead, it can eventually die of lead poisoning. An autopsy performed on several dead condors showed they died of lead poisoning. Since condors dine on carrion, the lead must have been in the carcass of the dead animals. But where did the lead come from?

1. The lead comes from the b __ l __ __ ts of h __ __ te __ __. Use the letters in SUN and RULE to fill in the blanks.

HAPPY RETURN

Biologists knew they had to do something to save the condors. To protect the remaining birds, the biologists set up a program known as captive breeding. This allowed wild condors to breed in captivity. As the population grew, birds were released back in the wild. In 1992, there were 63 condors. By 2002, the number increased to 198 condors. The recovery program cost $40 million.

2. How much of the $40 million did each bird represent?

3. Why do you think anyone would agree to spend large sums of money on a carrion-eating bird?

4. Use the capitalized letters in CaPTIvE bReediNg, plus an extra T and two O's to produce a word that describes what captive breeding provides for the California condor.

NOTHING'S PERFECT

Critics of the captive breeding program say many of the released condors die. They become overly tame; some are dying from poison produced from lead buckshot found in animal carcasses.

5. Many hunters say there isn't conclusive proof that ammunition is the source of lead poisoning in condors. Why do you think they believe this?

6. Add two vowels to letters two, three, four, and five in AMMUNITION to produce a word that means to protect against something harmful.

7. At the present time, the breed and release program costs more than $1 million a year. If the lead problem continues, do you think it makes sense to release condors from captivity? Why or why not?

BRAIN BUILDERS

Challenge Number One: Use eight letters to produce a California condor.

Challenge Number Two: Some people express sorrow for animals held in captivity. What four letters in CAPTIVITY spell a word that shows compassion?

74 **Rodent Roundup 1**

——Standard-Based Concept——

Lack of resources and other factors, such as disturbing the environment, force some species to find new habitats.

RODENT REVIEW

Rodents are gnawing animals with large front teeth (incisors). These common animals live in many places around the world. They eat leaves, stems, seeds, and roots. Some examples include gophers, squirrels, mice, and rats.

RAMBUNCTIOUS RAT

The rat is an unruly, long-tailed rodent. Rats can be very destructive pests and carriers of disease.

RODENT QUIZ

   1. Use the letter and word clues below to identify characteristics of rodents.

Clues

__ n __ __ s __ R __	type of front teeth
__ __ O __ s	rodents destroy these
D __ __ e __ s __	rodents carry these
E __ __ s	important organs
__ N __ __ i __ __	teeth action
__ __ a __ T __	food for rodents

2. Use the answers from Item 1 to fill in the blank spaces below.

   Rodents are _____ mammals. The two pairs of large front teeth are called _____. They have well-developed _____. They eat _____. Some damage _____ and carry _____.

BIG CITY RATS

Street rats, sewer rats, and roof rats . . . rats everywhere! A newspaper article recently reported an overpopulation of rats in New York City. Rodent experts advised against poisoning them. They said a better solution would be for people to limit the amount of _____ they toss in the garbage. Rats crave _____. It seems to give them the energy necessary to carry on their life activities.

3. The same word fits both empty spaces. The six letters needed to spell the word are circled in the sign. Unscramble the letters for the answer.

4. New York City held a Rat Summit to decide how to get rid of the rat problem. If you were holding the meeting, who would you invite to attend?

5. Write two or three suggestions you feel might help resolve the problem.

BRAIN BUILDERS

Challenge Number One: Rodents are vertebrates, animals with a backbone. Use the letters in VERTEBRATE to spell the names of two gnawing rodents, two mammals, and one insect.

Challenge Number Two: Every night for two weeks a mouse ate the cheese from Judy's trap. The trap didn't snap. Judy grew tired of spending money on cheese. So she devised a clever plan. Instead of using real cheese, she decided to put a picture of a hunk of cheese on the trap. What do you think Judy found on the trap the next day?

75 Rodent Roundup 2

──Standard-Based Concept──

Behavior is one kind of response an organism can make to environmental stimuli.

ROLE OF A VOLE

A vole, or meadow mouse, is a small rodent with a short tail. They live in grassland areas. They produce large numbers of young, often overpopulating their environment. Voles provide a food source for reptiles, birds, and mammals.

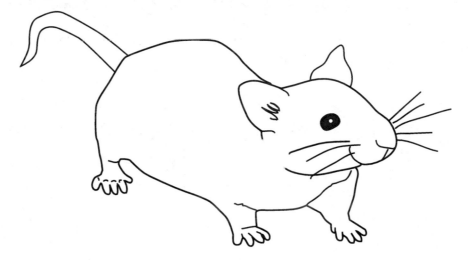

HOME PROBLEMS

Question: What happens to voles when they lose their homes? *Answer:* They find new ones. In 2001, residents in a northern California town complained of meadow mice invading their backyards and feasting in their gardens. Why are voles leaving their homes? Two things seem to be causing the problem:
A _____ _____ and the _____ of _____
_____. CLUES: weather, building.

1. Fill in the empty spaces with the words below. There are two extra words.

new	dirt	supply	mild
winter	construction	homes	

   The voles chewed up plants and grass, ate through sprinkler systems, and gnawed away on wooden decks.

What's Up in Science?

2. When voles lose their habitat, they need to find another home. Do you think they should be killed for this? Why or why not?

3. Some residents say the invading voles should be shot or poisoned. If this happens, what problems do you think might arise?

4. Some residents blame the city for the vole problem. They say the city allowed for too much building of homes, driving voles out of their burrows. Do you think this is a legitimate complaint? Why or why not?

5. Health officials told the residents that the vole problem was a natural event. It will solve itself in time. As a resident with a vole invasion, would you be satisfied to "wait out" the problem? Why or why not?

6. Voles can reproduce twenty-one days after being born. They may have five to ten litters a year. If 150 voles have eight litters a year, eight babies per litter, how many new voles will be born?

7. See how many voles you can create with the letters below. HINT: A trick looms.

> O M L A D O U E S L W
>
> E M O E V L E O V E O
>
> I can create _____ voles.

BRAIN BUILDERS

Challenge Number One: Think of a way to adjust the letters in VOLE to show an expression of affection.

Challenge Number Two: Use three letters in RATE, plus the letter P, to show one way to contain a vole.

76 The Smallest of Critters

——Standard-Based Concept——

Biological adaptations to an environment strengthen an organism's chance to survive and reproduce.

SIMPLY PRIMATES

Primates are mammals with flexible hands and feet. They have fingers on their hands and toes on their feet. Primate examples are lemurs, monkeys, apes, and humans.

A LOOK AT LEMURS

These small primates have thick hair, a pointed face, and a long tail. Most of them live on Madagascar, an island in the Indian Ocean off the southeast coast of Africa. They live in trees and feed at night.

PUT ON THE FEEDBAG

1. Lemurs eat a variety of plants and animals. Use the clues to help you identify the favorite food of some lemurs.

    Clues

    _ _ _ _ _ L _ _   snakes, for example; rhymes with smiles

    _ E _ _   turns into plants; sounds like greed

    M

    _ _ U _ _   plant product

    _ _ R _ _   need feathers to fly

ITTY-BITTY PRIMATE

The mouse lemur carries the title "world's smallest primate." This tiny animal weighs about one ounce. It lives on Madagascar. Sometimes life can be rough for the mouse lemur. It ranks high among the world's most endangered species.

2. A paper clip weighs about one gram. There are 28 grams in one ounce. If 30 mouse lemurs weigh 34.6 ounces, how many paper clips would it take to equal their weight?

3. An endangered species faces the risk of becoming extinct. What factor do you think contributes the most to an animal's chance of survival?

The Smallest of Critters *(continued)*

GOOD NEWS

In November 2002, scientists reported finding three new species of mouse lemurs on Madagascar. They say the discovery represents a "good sign."

4. What do you think a "good sign" or positive response might be from finding a new species of animal?

SMALL HAUL

In 2000, scientists found _____ of a primate. They claimed the primates lived 42 _____ years ago. The _____ creatures weighed from one-third of an ounce to one-half of an ounce. According to the scientists, the two-inch-long _____ are the smallest primates ever found. One group of _____ says the primates appeared on Earth 85 million years ago. Another group believes primates emerged 55 million years ago. The two _____ are 30 million years apart.

5. Unscramble the six terms below. Then fill the empty spaces with the terms that complete the sentences.

porgus   oliminl   alsmina
yitn   sitnectsis   sfsoils

BRAIN BUILDERS

Challenge Number One: Use the letters in LEMUR to spell the name of a pack animal, an Australian bird, and a snakelike fish. You may use a letter more than once.

Challenge Number Two: What letters in PRIMATE spell the name of a primate?

Challenge Number Three: Where would a human emotion appear *twice* in the following statement?

"Endanger means to face danger or harm."

Section 7

Life on Land and Water: Challenge Activities

1. Write a report on one of the following topics:

   - The discovery of Bigfoot in North America: Fake or real? Is there scientific evidence to support the find?

   - What have investigators done to prove or disprove the existence of the Loch Ness Monster?

2. Write ten true statements about the life cycle of a tapeworm.

3. Grasshoppers and crickets damage many acres of rich farmland. List several ways these destructive insects benefit an ecosystem.

4. At various times the grasshopper and cricket populations grow out of control. Describe some of the factors responsible for these large masses of insects.

5. Investigators believe many California condors died from lead poisoning. They say the lead came from animals shot by hunters. The condors ate the dead animals. Do you think there should be an emphasis on finding an alternative to lead ammunition? If so, use examples to support your position. If not, give two or three statements to back up your argument.

6. Present several reasons why new discoveries add to the pool of scientific knowledge.

7. There are two animals living in the same habitat. Animal X appears to be thriving and experiencing few problems. Animal Y may soon become extinct. Write a report describing the factors you think Animal Y might be facing.

8. Some people support the use of mice and other live animals for scientific research. Others believe the animals suffer at the hands of investigators. Write a report listing the pros and cons of using live animals for scientific study.

9. Research the federal guidelines outlining the proper handling of live animals in a science laboratory.

10. A six-foot-long sperm whale is a mammal. So is the tiny lemur. List and describe five characteristics of a mammal.

Section 8

What's Up in Genetic Science?

Section 8 presents eight activities featuring heredity—the transmission of traits, physical and others, from parent to offspring. The first activity serves as a review of genetic terms; the remaining exercises consider chromosome and gene study, genetic engineering, mutations, human stem cell controversy, the human genome, and cloning.

Several activities introduce the issue of modifying the genetic structure of plants and animals. These topics promote substantial debate, even within the scientific community. Food safety ranks high as a sensitive issue. Many scientists are concerned about genetic contamination of non-hybridization crops adapted to particular localities (e.g., Mexican "mountain" corn) or about genetically altered fish (e.g., salmon) interbreeding with wild species.

The puzzle exercises, open-ended questions, and brain builder activities in this section are designed to encourage students to use their creative and critical thinking skills. At the end of this section you will find a list titled Challenge Activities. These may serve as a reward for those students who desire extra credit.

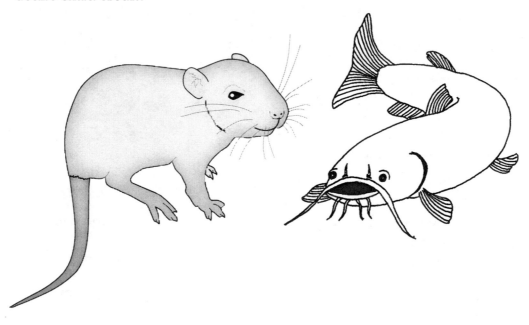

77 Genetic Review

——Standard-Based Concept——

The traits you inherit from your parents make you what you are. Genes are a set of instructions encoded in the DNA sequence of each organism.

WARMING UP

Activities 78 through 84 will involve genetics. Genetics is the study of heredity. Scientists who study heredity are called geneticists. Activity 77 will serve as a review of genetic terms used in the next seven activities.

CIRCLE TWENTY

1. There are twenty terms related to genetics scattered around the puzzle. Find and circle the terms in the puzzle. Terms may be up, down, forward, backward, or diagonal.

```
O  T  N  A  L  P  S  N  A  R  T  U  V  O
G  N  I  C  I  L  P  S  E  N  E  G  G  R
E  O  L  L  E  C  M  E  T  S  Y  O  E  P
N  I  G  E  N  O  L  C  I  P  L  I  N  C
O  T  R  A  I  T  M  H  A  S  N  S  E  E
M  A  I  R  E  G  O  R  P  O  O  A  T  L
I  T  S  L  E  C  E  O  G  Y  I  E  I  L
C  U  T  O  D  H  E  M  E  R  T  V  C  V
S  M  R  I  T  N  V  O  N  B  A  E  C  A
O  D  A  E  C  L  A  S  E  M  I  P  O  R
A  T  N  O  B  S  R  O  P  E  R  A  D  Y
P  E  D  G  E  N  E  M  A  P  A  L  E  R
G  E  A  E  M  O  N  E  G  T  V  K  S  M
```

gene	variation	cell
chromosome	genome	genetic code
DNA	gene map	genomics
progeria	transplant	encode
mutation	stem cell	strand
clone	gene therapy	gene splicing
trait	embryo	

Genetic Review *(continued)*

MATCHING

2. Write the terms from Item 1 next to their matching descriptions.

<u>Terms</u>

1. _____
2. _____
3. _____
4. _____
5. _____

6. _____

7. _____
8. _____
9. _____
10. _____
11. _____
12. _____
13. _____
14. _____

15. _____

16. _____

17. _____

18. _____
19. _____

20. _____

<u>Description</u>

1. Individual parts bound together.
2. The characteristics of an organism.
3. Important chemical found in chromosomes.
4. A change or alteration in the genetic code.
5. An organism carrying identical genes from its parent.
6. A bit of hereditary information; found in chromosomes.
7. Premature aging; a rare genetic disorder.
8. To transfer information or data into code.
9. The basic unit of life.
10. Early stage development of an organism.
11. To move body tissue from one place to another.
12. An embryonic cell used to cultivate other cells.
13. A display of the location of an organism's genes.
14. The difference between two similar organisms or structures.
15. DNA transfer from the genes of one organism to the genes of another organism.
16. Programs or projects based on genome research.
17. A DNA strand that carries the code for the inherited characteristics of an organism.
18. An organism's total genetic material.
19. The hereditary information from the parents carried by the genes. The blueprint for the features of an organism.
20. The treatment given to those with hereditary problems.

BRAIN BUILDERS

Challenge Number One: Heredity means the inheritance of traits. Traits are characteristics of an organism. See if you can find a trait in the word HEREDITY.

Challenge Number Two: Identical twins result from a single fertilized egg cell. The two individuals have identical hereditary makeup. Think of a way to produce identical twins using eight letters.

78 From One Gene to Another 1

—Standard-Based Concept—

Pairs of genes for traits are inherited from parents. Each parent contributes one gene for each trait to the offspring.

GENE THING

A gene is a unit of inheritance, a piece of information passed from parents to offspring. Two genes, one from each parent, determine a feature or trait. For example, hair color is a characteristic or trait an individual inherits from parents.

1. Make a list of six traits you inherited from your parents.

a. _____

b. _____

c. _____

d. _____

e. _____

f. _____

RAT ON

An Australian scientist recently identified a new gene. According to the researcher, the gene controls a person's desire for food. The gene came from a rat.

2. Why would a rat gene be compared to a human gene? It appears the rat gene is _____ to the human one. The letters scattered in the figure go together for the answer. Write the answer in the empty space.

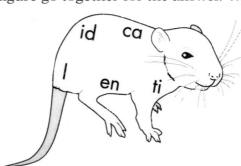

3. Experts say the new gene discovery could lead to the first gene-based drug to treat _____ and _____. Put the broken groups of letters together for the answers needed to fill the empty spaces.

dia   ty   si   bet   es   obe

LAB MONKEYS

Scientists use gene therapy to treat various illnesses. In 2000, an exciting event took place. An experimental drug injected into the brains of monkeys reversed the damage caused by Parkinson's disease.

Parkinson's disease is a human problem. There is gradual loss of muscle control. Muscle tremors or shakes make it difficult for people to eat or dress themselves. Monkeys do not naturally acquire Parkinson's. The scientists artificially induced the disease. Before the monkeys received the drug, they could barely move. After the injections, the monkeys regained their strength.

4. Why do you think scientists use monkeys in their experimental research?

The drug must be approved before it can be used on humans. This may take three to five years.

5. Why do you think it takes so long to gain approval?

BRAIN BUILDERS

Challenge Number One: Use seven letters in GENETICS to spell the names of organisms studied by an entomologist. You may use a letter more than once.

Challenge Number Two: Use four letters in HEREDITY to spell the name of a mammal.

79 From One Gene to Another 2

—Standard-Based Concept—

Changes in DNA (mutations) occur spontaneously at low rates. Some of these changes make no difference to the organism, whereas others can change cells and organisms.

TOUGH WORK AHEAD

Scientists are currently working on ways to treat problems plaguing humans. Lab animals help researchers find clues to unravel many of the mysteries hidden within the genes. For many years scientists have used a variety of animals for inbreeding and selective breeding. Inbreeding refers to the crossing of closely related organisms. In selective breeding, two animals mate to produce offspring with unique features.

1. Identify eight organisms in the puzzle that geneticists use for chromosome and gene study. The clues will help you fill in the blank spaces.

	Clues
_ O _ _ _ _	rat, for example
_ R _ _ t fly	winged insect
G _ _ _ _ _ pig	small, tailless rodent
_ A _	member of feline group
_ _ N _ _ _	long-tailed primate
_ I _	curly-tailed swine
S _ _ _ _	wooly critter
_ _ M _ _	a person

2. There are four conditions or diseases hidden "within the genes." Circle the letters that spell the name of each condition or disease. Begin at the top and move from left to right. CLUE: The answers begin with letters h, d, o, and P.

geneheargenIngegloensse

genedIagebetneesgene

geobenesIgentyegene

genepagerkInnesonsgene

Copyright © 2004 by John Wiley & Sons, Inc.

From One Gene to Another 2 *(continued)*

MUTATE STATE

3. A mutation occurs when the structure of a gene or chromosome changes. _____, a rare disorder that turns children into old people, results from a single misplaced DNA molecule. The eight numbered spaces correspond to the letters of the English alphabet. For example, A = 1, B = 2, and so forth. Replace the numbers with letters and write the word in the empty space.

   —   —   —   —   —   —   —   —

   16   18   15   7   5   18   9   1

4. One person with the disease (Answer to Item 3) is born each year in the United States. How important is it for researchers to find a way to correct the problem in the mutant genes? Explain your answer.

5. Change within an organism's genetic code may lead to a mutation. _____ and _____ are known to cause mutations. The letters needed to spell the missing words are scattered below. Put them together and fill in the empty spaces. HINT: The answers sound like tentacles and plugs.

   h u   a   s   m   r
       c   g   l   s   c   i   d   e

BRAIN BUILDERS

Challenge Number One: What does **g**, upside down **e**, **n**, and upside down **e** combine to form?

Challenge Number Two: Use the letters in CHROMOSOME to spell the names of two different mammals. You may use a letter more than once.

80 Designer Catfish

⸺Standard-Based Concept⸺

Genetic engineering involves the transfer of genes, or segments of DNA, from one organism to another. Certain traits carried by the transferred genes are passed on to future generations.

SOMETHING ABOUT CATFISH

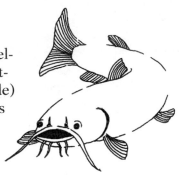

Catfish have a torpedo-shaped body and long fleshy feelers (known as barbells) around the mouth and chin. Catfish carry spines on their dorsal (top) and pectoral (side) fins. These act as defense weapons. They have small eyes and no scales covering their body. Many people enjoy catching and eating catfish.

NEW FISH IN TOWN

Several years ago, the walking catfish came to Florida from Asia. Tropical fish dealers brought them to the U.S. They kept them in local ponds. After a short time the catfish escaped. They were able to shimmy their bodies and use their spines to "walk" to nearby _____
and _____. The catfish can
_____ air. Unfortunately, the walking catfish posed a big problem. They ate too many _____
fish. The people responsible for bringing the catfish to America made a costly
_____.

1. The missing words are hidden in the puzzle. Find and circle them. Then fill in the empty spaces with the correct words from top to bottom. Answers may be forward or backward.

F	C	A	N	A	L	S	O	S
L	R	S	R	E	V	I	R	I
O	E	H	T	A	E	R	B	O
E	N	A	T	I	V	E	T	L
R	E	K	A	T	S	I	M	E

2. Sometimes problems arise when you least expect them. For example, the walking catfish nearly wiped out the local fish population. What do you think the tropical fish dealers should have done before bringing in the walking catfish?

Copyright © 2004 by John Wiley & Sons, Inc.

GENETIC ENGINEERING

Scientists stay busy searching for ways to make life better. Technology plays a strong role in their quest for improvement. Technology includes transferring DNA from the genes of one organism to the genes of another organism. Some people think science has gone too far.

3. How do you feel about genetic engineering? Do you believe the majority of people will be helped by it? Why or why not?

A CATFISH CAPER

4. In 2001, a university researcher in Alabama experimented with channel catfish. He transferred DNA from salmon, carp, and zebrafish into the catfish. This caused the catfish to _____ _____. Use the following clues to help you find the missing words. HINT: The first word rhymes with dough; the second word sounds like disaster.

Small   →   BIG

(six months earlier)   (one year later)

FAT CATS

According to the report, the catfish grew 60 percent faster than normal. Federal officials feared the channel catfish, like their walking catfish cousin, might create problems in the environment.

5. If the catfish entered local waterways, how might they wreak havoc with the environment? List two possible problems.

a. _____

_____

b. _____

_____

BRAIN BUILDERS

Challenge Number One: How can you "alter" the word GENETIC to make it more vigorous?

Challenge Number Two: How can you "alter" the word GENETIC to make it common?

81 Biotech Foods

——Standard–Based Concept——

Technology provides science with the tools for investigation, inquiry, and analysis.

GMOs

GMO stands for "genetically modified organisms." Such foods as soybeans, corn, and canola plants have been modified or altered. According to scientists, these plants resist certain herbicides or diseases when altered. Some people refuse to eat any foods with GMO ingredients. They say the altered foods might make them sick. These products are also referred to as biotech foods.

1. The names of three crop plants scientists alter are
   _____ (stiruf), _____
   (tevebgsela), and _____ (wetah). Unscramble
   the words in parentheses and write them in the empty spaces.

CAUGHT IN THE MIDDLE

In 1998, U.S. midwestern corn and soybean farmers lost large sums of money. Much of their crops were exported to Europe. Many of the European people refused to eat engineered food. Asian food manufacturers joined with the Europeans. They, too, chose not to use GMOs. Interestingly, the same Asian markets accepted meat produced from livestock known to have eaten biotech grains.

Many U.S. farmers continue to plant altered seeds. These seeds produce higher yields of crops. Some farmers have stopped growing biotech plants. They returned to growing non-biotech crops to avoid losing profits.

2. Use the clues to help you fill in
   the spaces in the puzzle with
   terms related to biotech foods.

ACROSS:

2. To change or modify.
4. Ears of a cereal plant.
5. The origin of new plants.

DOWN:

1. Chemical known to destroy plants.
3. The use of technology in studying
   organisms.

HINT: All puzzle terms appear on this
   activity.

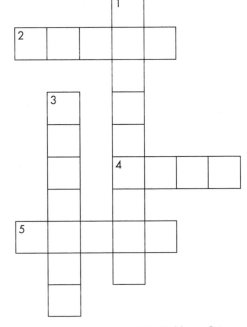

3. Would you refuse to eat engineered food? Why or why not?

DANDY DEBATE

Supporters of GMOs say the increase of food production will help to reduce world hunger. Critics view GMOs as large-scale business run by U.S. farmers. At the present time, the opponents of altered foods believe the U.S. is doing very little to benefit developing countries.

In June 2003, about two thousand demonstrators swarmed downtown Sacramento, California. They were protesting the U.S. government's role at an international agriculture conference. They claimed the U.S. government wants to take over the worldwide food system. They protested the "dangerous practice of genetically engineered food." A report (2003) by the American Medical Association states at least forty varieties of genetically altered crops are currently in use. To date, no ill effects on human health or the environment have been detected since modified foods first hit the market less than ten years ago. Protestors say the conference is not about world hunger, but to promote U.S. technology. Police arrested over forty demonstrators during the three-day conference.

4. At what point do you think protestors get out of control?

5. Do you think police handle protestors in a rough manner? Why or why not?

BRAIN BUILDERS

Challenge Number One: Use four different letters in MONEY CROP to write the name of a money crop.

Challenge Number Two: Show three ways to alter a seed.

82 Human Stem Cells

──Standard–Based Concept──

Societal challenges inspire questions for scientific research. Social attitudes and pressures often determine the availability of funding for research.

STEM CELLS

Stem cells form soon after fertilization. They are referred to as embryonic stem cells. These are cells in an early stage of development. Stem cells are able to develop into various cell types in the body. Researchers have made nerve cells (neurons), heart cells, and muscle cells from stem cell tissue. They have also made cells of cartilage, bone, and skin from stem cell material.

Stem cell biology holds a bright future for people suffering from illness. Scientists are hard at work searching for new ways to use stem cells to replace or repair damage or diseased body parts.

1. Complete the names of various damaged or diseased tissue that stem cells might replace or repair. Use the clues in parentheses to help you.

   a. c _ r _ i _ c   (heart)
   b. c _ r _ e _   (eye structure)
   c. p _ n _ r _ a _   (produces insulin)
   d. m _ s _ l _   (movement)
   e. c _ r _ i _ a _ e   (gristle-like tissue)
   f. l _ v _ r   (secretes bile)
   g. b _ a _ n   (cranium)
   h. c _ t _ n _ o _ s   (refers to skin)

YES OR NO

Many people around the world do not support stem cell research. They object because human embryos must be destroyed in order to collect their stem cells. An embryo contains about 100 cells five days after fertilization. Most of these are stem cells. Removal of stem cells kills the embryo. Some people fear researchers will use stem cells to grow organs or other body parts. Others believe scientists might attempt to clone a human being.

2. Are you in favor of human stem cell research? Why or why not?

There is much controversy over the issue of embryonic stem cells. Some American scientists believe the United States government is too strict in regulating human stem cell research. A few researchers have moved to Great Britain to continue their work. The British government supports the cloning of stem cells from human embryos.

3. Express your opinion regarding each of the following statements:

   a. Human stem cells should only be used to treat illnesses.

   b. Some people believe life starts at conception (the beginning of an embryo). Destroying an embryo to attain stem cells is the same thing as murder.

   c. Most embryos needed for research are grown artificially in fertility clinics. Therefore, people shouldn't object to stem cell study.

   d. Some people say adult stem cells from blood and bone marrow produce results similar to those of embryonic stem cells. Researchers should use only adult stem cells.

   e. The federal government needs to fund human stem cell research. Without government backing, research will slow down. People may die as a result of limited research.

BRAIN BUILDERS

Challenge Number One: Think of a way to produce a male offspring from an embryo.

Challenge Number Two: Six letters from STEM CELL TISSUE combine to spell the name of a body tissue produced from stem cell tissue. What is it?

83 Human Genome

─Standard-Based Concept─

Genes are a set of instructions encoded in the DNA sequence of each organism. A genome is the total genetic makeup of an organism.

ALL THE WAY WITH DNA

In 2000, a biotech company reported it had decoded the genome or total genetic material of a human being. This means scientists mapped or made a blueprint of millions of DNA fragments. The report covers about 90 percent of the human genome.

1. What do geneticists hope to gain from studying the human genome? For the answer, complete the blanks from words listed below. Five words do not apply.

   a. The research may help _____ scientists combat _____ illnesses.

   b. The research may provide new _____ for various _____.

   c. The research may find ways to _____ the effects of aging.

ailments	organism
genetics	prevent
increase	sequence
major	tissue
medical	treatments

WHAT'S UP WITH THAT?

Study data suggest humans have only three times as many genes as a fruit fly. Research also indicates humans may have only a few hundred more genes than a mouse.

2. Based on this information, we are more than our genes. Why do you think humans are at the top of the evolutionary ladder? In other words, what makes us unique?

What's Up in Science?

GATHERING GENES

The human genome report stated the human genetic code was made up of about 30,000 genes. At the present time, nobody can say for sure how many genes are in the human body. New findings place the number of genes at _____ or more. Not all study groups use the same method for collecting data. As a result, the total estimate of the number of genes will vary.

3. To complete the statement above, you'll need to solve the following problem:

    (a) Multiply 365.7 by 26.4. _____

    (b) Multiply the answer by 20. _____

    (c) Subtract 103,089.60 from answer (b). _____

PROBLEM ZONE

Information regarding the human genome may present a problem for some people. Genetic tests identify people who are at risk of developing certain diseases. Reports indicate that questions about genetic diseases appear on some job applications. Some workers claim they lost their jobs because of genetic problems in their families.

4. Do you think companies should use personal genetic data when hiring employees? Why or why not?

BIG ANNOUNCEMENT

In Spring 2003, scientists reported 99 percent completion of the human genome project. Now the work begins on how the DNA information directs the _____ (wgohrt), _____ (file), _____ (oucdornpitre), _____ (sedasies), and _____ (thead) of human beings.

5. Unscramble the letters in parentheses and write the answers in the empty spaces above.

BRAIN BUILDERS

Challenge Number One: Think of a way to get "one gem" of a person from a genome.

Challenge Number Two: Edna and Dan were discussing genetics. Edna said to Dan, "Did you know I'm three-fourths DNA?" Dan replied, "Not good enough. I'm 100 percent DNA." How could Dan support his statement?

84 What About Cloning?

—Standard-Based Concept—

Societal challenges inspire questions for scientific research. Social attitudes and pressures often determine the availability of funding for research.

MIRROR IMAGE

A clone is a group of genetically identical cells. These cells develop into an entire new organism. The organism is genetically identical to its parent.

1. Sketch a clone for each organism below.

GOODBYE, DOLLY

Dolly, the famous cloned sheep, died in February 2003, from a lung disease. She lived six years. Dolly was the result of an altered adult sheep cell growing inside a surrogate mother sheep. A surrogate acts as a substitute for the real parent. It took almost 250 tries to produce Dolly.

2. According to scientists, Dolly represents people's efforts to master and control the molecular details of life. What do you think this statement means?

SAY CHEESE

Since 1997, scientists have been busy cloning mice, pigs, cows, and a cat. Many of these animals died before birth; some showed abnormal development.

3. Problems arise from cloning animals. Do you believe cloning should continue or stop? Defend your answer.

What About Cloning? (continued)

HEE HAW

In 2003, scientists reported the birth of a cloned baby mule. The mule marks the first time a genetic carbon copy of an equine (horse-like) animal has been created. To date, scientists have failed to clone dogs, monkeys, and horses.

4. Let's have some make-believe fun. A fictitious person, Dr. Bugby, rocked the science world by cloning five different insects. Identify each of them by supplying the missing letters in their names.

$$C \_\_ C \_\_ \_\_ T$$
$$\_\_ E \_\_ \_\_ L E$$
$$\_\_ O \_\_ H$$
$$\_\_ N \_\_$$
$$H \_\_ \_\_ E \_\_ B \_\_ E$$

CLONING CONCERNS

Some cloned animals—mice, sheep, and cows—produce oversized fetuses; others experience physical problems, such as abnormal growths. Scientists say a certain gene changes the way a fetus grows and causes defects in the animals.

Two types of cloning exist—reproductive and therapeutic. Reproductive cloning attempts to duplicate a person. Therapeutic cloning creates cells needed for research. These cells would be used to treat injuries and diseases. According to a recent survey, the majority of Americans oppose cloning because they feel it is morally wrong. A significant number believe the science is not yet safe enough.

5. In Spring 2003, the House of Representatives voted 241 to 155 to ban human cloning. Do you think the government will permit human cloning some time in the future? Why or why not?

BRAIN BUILDERS

Challenge Number One: Use three different letters in CLONED to write the name of an animal that may some day be cloned.

Challenge Number Two: Find letters in CLONED to write a word that expresses a negative response to human cloning.

Section 8

What's Up in Genetic Science?
Challenge Activities

1. Describe what you think would be the "perfect" plant. If you had the technology to grow such a plant, list the traits you would want the plant to have.

2. Write a one-page report describing Walter Sutton's chromosome theory.

3. List ten true statements regarding DNA.

4. Research how DNA plays a vital role in the forensic laboratory.

5. Describe the work done by genetic counselors.

6. Research three genetic disorders and write a report describing the problems brought on by each disorder.

7. Give the advantages and disadvantages of inbreeding.

8. Read the following passage. Then write a one- or two-paragraph response to each of the listed items.

   Scientists are attempting to clone endangered species and recently extinct animals. Some of the animals include the Spanish mountain goat, Tasmanian tiger, giant panda, and Asian gaur (wild ox). Many scientists believe cloning technology will lead the way in saving animals. Some people feel cloning will create additional problems.

   a. Cloning could play an important role in the preservation of species.

   b. An extinct species may return to an unfamiliar environment. This could cause more harm than good.

   c. A cloned animal may not be strong enough to survive.

   d. Many cloning attempts fail. Besides, this is not an ethical way to create life.

   e. If we placed more stress on saving habitats, then there would be less need to clone endangered species.

Section 9

Timely Real-Life Topics of Concern

Section 9 offers seven activities that ask students to examine several passages touching on real-life issues. Students read the concerns, state the problem, and write two comments or suggestions expressing their opinions regarding each issue.

The topics in this section promote lively debates and bring people together to work on resolving the issues. Some of the problems may take years to solve; others may take only a short time.

As you know, real-life events happen on a regular basis. And, of course, as controversial topics emerge, people will continue to express their views and ideas. The challenge of problem solving is an ongoing process.

The topics of concern allow critical thinkers to study the issue, make careful observations, and develop and deliver intelligent responses.

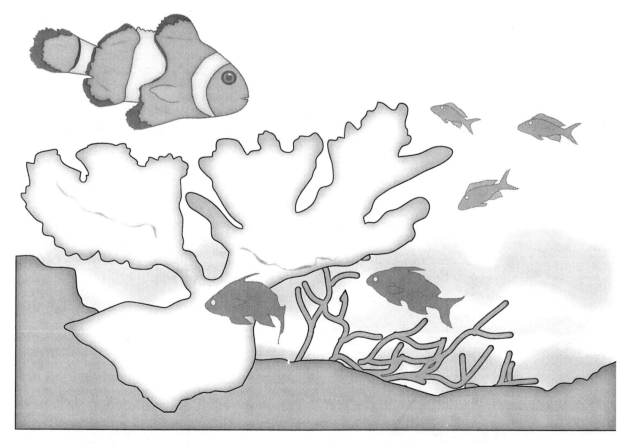

85 Environmental Pollution 1

——Standard-Based Concept——

Maintaining environmental health involves establishing or monitoring quality standards related to use of soil, water, and air.

PROCEDURE

Read the three real-life environmental pollution issues. In the space below each issue, state the problem; then write two comments or suggestions.

A. DRILLING FOR OIL

Oil companies want to drill for oil in the Arctic region of North America. Many people and wildlife species depend on the Arctic coastal plain for existence. Supporters of drilling operations claim that 16 billion barrels of oil lie under the coastal plain. The opposite view points to only about 3.2 billion barrels. Opponents say oil companies damage the land. They ruin the landscape and create toxic spills.

Problem:

Comments or Suggestions:

1.

2.

B. ENERGY CRISIS

Power plants work harder and longer during an energy crisis. Consumer demand runs high and plant personnel keep moving at a fast pace. The older plants using fossil fuels—natural gas, oil, and coal—to produce energy heavily pollute the air. Many plants exceed pollution limits to supply the needed energy.

Problem:

Comments or Suggestions:

1.

2.

C. WORLD WAR II WEAPONS DUMPING

After World War II, British and Soviet troops dumped German bombs and chemicals into the Baltic Sea. According to scientists, saltwater broke down or corroded the weapon casings. Poisons like arsenic, mustard gas, and sarin leaked from the canisters. Some experts believe the poisons can enter the food chain and spread to different sea organisms. Some military personnel say it might be best to leave the discarded weapons alone. Trying to recover the weapons might cause toxic material to escape and cause widespread concern. Besides, it would cost millions of dollars to retrieve the weapons from the sea floor.

Problem:

Comments or Suggestions:

1.

2.

86 Environmental Pollution 2

─Standard–Based Concept─

Environmental problems and resource depletion vary from region to region and from country to country.

PROCEDURE

Read the two real-life environmental pollution issues. In the space below each issue, state the problem; then write two comments or suggestions on how you think the problem might be handled.

A. CRUISE SHIP POLLUTION

Protestors cry out, "The California coastline needs to be protected." The protestors claim cruise ships dump sewage, oily bilge water, and toxic chemicals into the sea. They say the laws are too lenient. The Cruise Industry Association agreed to stop disposing of sewage and wastewater within four miles of the coast.

Problem:

Comments or Suggestions:

1.

2.

B. BIG POLLUTERS GO FREE

A recent report by the Environmental Protection Agency (EPA) stated that large industrial plants violate pollution laws. Based on the report, few of the plants receive fines or penalties. The report found that one-half of the biggest offenders exceed pollution limits by more than 100 percent.

Problem:

Comments or Suggestions:

1.

2.

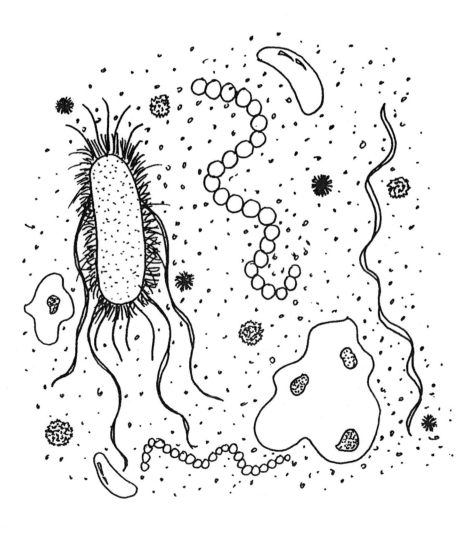

87 The Decreasing Fish Population

Standard-Based Concept

Pollution and over-fishing are threats to sea life. If too many species die, the entire ecosystem may collapse.

PROCEDURE

Read the three real-life issues on pollution and over-fishing. In the space below each issue, state the problem; then write two comments or suggestions on how you think the problem might be handled.

A. EFFICIENT FISHING

In 2003, a report, using data collected from the past fifty years, indicated that ocean fish are gradually being wiped out. A high percentage of cod, halibut, tuna, and swordfish are disappearing. Industrial fishing techniques catch fish by the thousands. If the trend continues, there could be a world-wide seafood shortage.

Problem:

Comments or Suggestions:

1.

2.

B. TOO MANY RESTRICTIONS

Some say the government should ease up on its approach to over-fishing. According to those close to the fishing industry, laws are already in place to address commercial fishing levels. There are regulations set to support the restoration of depleted stock.

Problem:

Comments or Suggestions:

1.

2.

C. POLLUTION IS A PROBLEM TOO

As more people move to coastal areas, more pollutants enter the sea. Runoff, water from streets and roadways, carries pollutants into the ocean. Estuaries and bays lose oxygen as a result of dissolved nutrients from runoff. These conditions do great harm to ocean life environments.

Problem:

Comments or Suggestions:

1.

2.

88 **Whale Concerns 1**

Standard-Based Concept

Human activities can disrupt an organism's environment and reduce its ability to survive.

PROCEDURE

Read the three real-life issues regarding whales. In the space below each issue, state the problem; then write two comments or suggestions on how you think the problem might be handled.

A. WHALE ROUNDUP

In 2000, a report stated the Japanese government broke an agreement. According to the report, Japan decided to hunt whales protected under an international law on commercial whale hunts. Foreign government officials and environmental groups say the Japanese hunt whales for food, not for scientific research.

Problem:

Comments or Suggestions:

1.

2.

B. WHALE SNACKS

The Japanese have hunted whales for more than a thousand years. Many Japanese citizens consider eating whale meat an important part of their culture. After World War II, the Japanese government supplied its people with whale meat. It kept many of them from starving to death.

Problem:

Comments or Suggestions:

1.

2.

C. HOLD YOUR FIRE

Can powerful air guns kill or injure whales? Environmental groups believe a research vessel using air guns to map the seafloor caused the death of two beaked whales. This happened in 2002 near the southern tip of Baja California. Part of the Marine Mammal Protection Act bans behavior believed to disturb marine mammals. However, the research team said there was no proof their work caused the whales' deaths.

Problem:

Comments or Suggestions:

1.

2.

89 Whale Concerns 2

——Standard-Based Concept——

Technology used to gather data adds strength and accuracy to scientific discoveries. At times, however, it can create problems for certain organisms.

PROCEDURE

Read the three real-life issues regarding whales. In the space below each issue, state the problem; then write two comments or suggestions on how you think the problem might be handled.

A. MORE WHALES DIE

In 2002, sixteen beaked whales beached themselves in the Bahamas. More whales died in the Canary Islands in September 2002. Environmentalists said the U.S. Navy's low-frequency sonic wave system caused injuries to the whales. The sonar system is used to detect enemy submarines. The whale deaths prompted a judge to stop the Navy from using the sonar. The Navy can begin testing again when environmental experts and Navy personnel make an agreement. They must agree on areas where the sonar can be used without harming marine life.

Problem:

Comments or Suggestions:

1.

2.

B. DEBATE IN ICELAND

Some people in Iceland want to resume hunting whales. Others believe whale hunts will hurt tourism. Visitors come to Iceland to watch whales play in their habitat. Tourism brings in money and casts a positive image for Iceland. The killing of whales might tarnish the image and chase the tourists away.

What's Up in Science?

Problem:

Comments or Suggestions:

1.

2.

C. BYCATCH BLUES

In 2003, a study reported nearly one thousand whales, dolphins, and porpoises drown every day. They become trapped in commercial fishing nets. Scientists say fishing nets may be the biggest immediate threat to these marine mammals. (Bycatch refers to accidental or unplanned killing by commercial fishermen.) Can something be done to address the bycatch problem? According to a recent report, the Mexican tuna fleet reduced the dolphin death rate by 90 percent.

Problem:

Comments or Suggestions:

1.

2.

90 Dealing with Dolphins

——Standard-Based Concept——

Certain aquatic mammals such as sea lions and dolphins serve as prey in the food chain. Predators capture and feed on other animals. The shark is an example of an aquatic predator.

PROCEDURE

Read the three real-life marine mammal issues. In the space below each issue, state the problem; then write two comments or suggestions on how you think the problem might be handled.

A. FREE SWIM

A Hawaiian tourist marvels at the grace and beauty of an energetic dolphin. Some business owners express an interest in bringing dolphins to local shopping malls. These mammals are the focus of a growing entertainment industry. Some people feel tourists might enjoy watching the mammals play as they shop for the latest tee-shirts.

Problem:

Comments or Suggestions:

1.

2.

B. SWIM WITH DOLPHINS?

In Oahu, Hawaii, visitors look forward to grabbing a tan or snorkeling the jagged coral reefs. A good number of tourists want to jump in the ocean and swim with the dolphins. FACT: Dolphins provide food for sharks.

In 2001, boat captains reported seeing sharks attack spinner dolphins. In June 2003, a man was bitten on his foot while swimming with a group of dolphins. Oahu's Shark Task Force is struggling with how best to warn swimmers. If they issue a strong warning, then tourists may choose to stay away. Local business would suffer. Regardless, swimmers need to be aware of the danger. Once a swimmer enters the water, he or she becomes part of the food chain.

Problem:

Comments or Suggestions:

1.

2.

C. PERFORMANCE IN THE PARK

In summer 2003, twenty-eight dolphins captured off the Solomon Islands (South Pacific Ocean, East of New Guinea) wound up in Cancun, Mexico. The dolphins joined other animals in an aquatic park. Animal activists feared the mammals wouldn't survive the long trip. They were concerned the dolphins might not do well in their new home.

The majority of parks use only dolphins bred in captivity. According to observers, the dolphins appeared healthy in their new environment.

Problem:

Comments or Suggestions:

1.

2.

91 **The Cold Facts About Cryonics**

─────**Standard-Based Concept**─────

Technology provides science with the tools for investigation, inquiry, and analysis.

PROCEDURE

Read the three real-life issues regarding cryonics. In the space below each issue, state the problem; then write two comments or suggestions on how you think the problem might be handled.

A. ICE PAC

Cryonics is the practice of freezing a human body. There are those who believe the preserved body can be revived some time in the future. Let's say a person dies from Disease Y. Fifty years after the person's death scientists find a cure for the disease. The theory holds that the person may be thawed out, revived, and the disease removed from the body. Happily, the individual receives a fresh start in life.

Problem:

Comments or Suggestions:

1.

2.

B. BASEBALL LEGEND

In 2003, baseball great Ted Williams passed away. A report stated that his body was frozen at a cryonics laboratory in Arizona. According to the report, there were plans to sell the DNA from his remains. The idea was to clone the cells in hopes of producing an individual with super athletic ability.

Problem:

Comments or Suggestions:

1.

2.

C. DOUBLE TROUBLE

Here's one for the imagination. The year: 2096. Scientists successfully clone the cells of a person who died in 2004. The cells develop into a duplicate human being. What a marvelous event! The "newly born" individual receives a second chance to live again.

Problem:

Comments or Suggestions:

1.

2.

Riddles for the Asking

The following riddles are waiting for those of you brave enough to tackle a puzzling question or statement. If you mix ingenuity with imagination, you'll usually succeed in solving a riddle or two. Several riddles are listed under each section title and match the theme of the unit.

Section 1: Preserved Evidence of Past Life

1. What did the boy clam fossil say to the girl clam fossil?

2. Where do some fossils sleep at night?

3. How does the thought of becoming a fossil affect trees?

4. What has no tongue, no lips, and no larynx, but can tell us about ancient life?

5. What did the fossil crab say to the fossil coral?

Section 2: Early Human Life on Earth

6. What was the favorite gum of early human hunters?

7. What did they call an early human without an appetite?

8. Why did early humans walk on two feet?

9. What was the favorite sandwich of early man?

10. Where did early human hunters celebrate at night?

Riddles for the Asking *(continued)*

Section 3: Getting to Know the Lithosphere

11. What do you call a competition between two volcanoes?

12. What do seismologists use to hold up their pants?

13. What part of an earthquake does the most damage?

14. How do seismologists seal an agreement?

15. What is the most circular part of a rock?

16. Why do some earthquakes only last for a few seconds?

17. Where do seismologists gather for meetings?

18. What solid piece of volcanic lava is part of a fairy tale?

Section 4: Listening to the Environment

19. Why did the boy put a model globe in the refrigerator?

20. Where would you find the most difficult part of a drought?

21. Why did the man decide to paint his house green?

22. Why is an ant a large part of the pollution problem?

Riddles for the Asking *(continued)*

Section 5: Ocean Features and Related Creatures

23. Why won't a jellyfish ever amount to much?

24. Why did the whale call the jellyfish a coward?

25. Where do baby whales go to eat?

26. What group of sea organisms sing all the time?

27. Why can't you trust a sea lion?

28. How can you prevent a sea lion from stealing your fishing bait?

Section 6: What's Happening in Space?

29. Where can you find stars made of solid matter?

30. What do you call a celebration sponsored by a cluster of stars?

31. What does a meteor need to become a meteorite?

32. What connects the first and second halves of a meteorite?

33. What space object mimics the sound a cow makes?

Riddles for the Asking *(continued)*

Section 7: Life on Land and Water

34. If a predator loses its teeth, what will it become?

35. Why did the weirdo bring a dead animal on the airplane with him?

36. Why don't crows ever become roadkill?

37. Where would you find a "negative" ant?

38. What part of a lemur describes a bird?

39. What part of a salamander is the most human?

Section 8: What's Up in Genetic Science?

40. What part of a catfish do people prefer to eat?

41. What two words in catfish describe how people catch them?

42. What career did Gene Ticist's parents want him to pursue?

43. I'm a home for genes and related things. What am I?

44. I'll give you red hair to start things off, then work to make your skin so soft. What am I?

45. I'm so confused and far from home, please tell me what number hides in a clone.

Answer Key

Section 1: Preserved Evidence of Past Life

1. What Fossils Have to Say

1. whale **2.** ear bone **3.** (1) clavicle, (2) femur, (3) patella, (4) sternum. **4.** Five of the letters spell mouse. BRAIN BUILDERS: Challenge Number One: ice age; Challenge Number Two: Use 4 letters from fossil—s,o,i,l—to spell soil.

2. Long-Ago Life Forms

1. Answers may vary. Students may say squirrels, snakes, rats, worms, and so forth. **2.** They know the age of the rocks containing the fossil tunnels. **3.** W–Wiggly, O—Organs, R—Round, M—Marine, S—Soil, Silt, or Sand. **4.** The burrow holes have the same diameter throughout each tunnel. BRAIN BUILDERS: Challenge Number One: t-u-n-n-e-l; Challenge Number Two: PORE.

3. Footprints from the Past

1. Statements in proper order: 1. Several dinosaurs are present. 2. They seek food along a river bank or lake shoreline. 3. They step in soft mud and sink. 4. They plod through mud and leave footprints behind. 5. A mixture of sand and water covers the prints. 6. Layers of mud, clay, or rock build up over the prints. 7. The mixture turns into cement and hardens. 8. Millions of years pass by. 9. Fossilized footprints form in sedimentary rock.

2. Mostly that millions of years ago a prehistoric beast lived in the area where the footprints were found. **3.** instep, heel, claw, toe. **4.** Beginning to speed up and move at a faster pace. BRAIN BUILDERS: Challenge Number One: SAND. Challenge Number Two: SUN.

4. Early Wings

1. Answers will vary. It is possible that birds evolved from an earlier reptile if the time scale proves to be accurate. Also, if scientists agree that the early reptile had feathers. **2.** Answers will vary. Scientists believe the feathers may have helped the reptile glide from place to place. **3.** Answers will vary. It might be enough evidence if the time line proves to be accurate. **4.** radius, lower arm. **5.** mandible, head. BRAIN BUILDERS: Challenge Number One: It is nearly ten inches long (9.96 inches). Challenge Number Two: SOIL.

5. Two Steps Ahead of the Rest

1. Fossils in rocks undergoing cuts and blasts have little chance of staying in one piece.   **2.** The fossil was fragile and needed to be handled with care. It represented an important piece of historical geology.
3. Drawings will vary.   **4.** 290 million years old.   **5.** Nobody knows for sure. It remains a great mystery. BRAIN BUILDERS: Challenge Number One: femur, vertebrae, skull, clavicle. Challenge Number Two: Remove "iz" from lizard and you'll have lard or hog fat.

6. Dinosaur-Snacking Crocodile

1. Super Croc may have run out of food, failed to adapt to a changing environment, contracted a deadly disease, met with a catastrophic event, and so on.   **2.** (Left to right, top to bottom) Top Line—TRICERATOPS (spelled backward)—a long horn above each eye, a short horn on the nose. Top Line—STEGOSAURUS—carries heavy bony plates on its back. Bottom Line—BRONTOSAUR—a 30-ton reptile. Bottom Line—TYRANNOSAURUS (spelled backward)—the "rex" part of the name is missing.   **3.** There are many fossils in the area.   **4.** It provided a big structure for detecting odors. Super Croc was probably able to smell an enemy or a dead carcass some distance away.   **5.** The scutes, like solar panels on the roof of a house, collect the sun's energy, thus providing a source of heat. BRAIN BUILDERS: Challenge Number One: The capital letters spell SUPER CROC. The small letters spell dinosaur. The combined letters indicate that SUPER CROC ate a dinosaur. Challenge Number Two: The 40-foot Super Croc measures 40 feet or 480 inches. A student 4 feet 6 inches would measure 54 inches. It would take 9 students to equal the length of Super Croc (54 times 9 equals 486 inches).

7. Awesome Dinosaur

1. Head and neck sketches will vary. Here's one possibility:

2. Plant, "beef," operate, frame.   **3.** "thunder reptile." The size of the Apatosaurus. . .   **4.** The giant reptile gained more than 30 pounds a day at the peak of its growth spurt.   **5.** Apatosaurus would gain approximately 3,150 pounds. Multiply the days in an average month (30) by 105 (3.5 times 30). Then multiply 30 (pounds per day) by 105 days. BRAIN BUILDERS: Challenge Number One: Sn is the atomic symbol for tin + c + (2+2=4) = is + x + ever + shun. They would go together like this: x + tin + c + shun (tion) + is + 4 (for) + ever. Challenge Number Two: teeny.

8. Even More Dinosaurs

1. 7 ounces = 0.44 lb; 0.44 lb divided by 80,000 lbs = 0.0000055 percent.
2. Large meteorite. **3.** Humans did not live during the Age of Dinosaurs.
4. Sketches will vary. Here's one possibility:

5. Argentinosaurus. BRAIN BUILDERS: Challenge Number One:
a. SOUND b. AIR. Challenge Number Two: ZOO.

9. Mast from the Past

1. Accept any reasonable answer. Scientists think the mastodon used its huge size and tusks to fight off enemies. Students should shade in the entire figure. **2.** Climate, grassland, food, water. **3.** Answers will vary. **4.** Saber-toothed cat, triceratops, trilobite, woolly mammoth, plesiosaurus, stegosaurus. BRAIN BUILDERS: Challenge Number One: TON. Challenge Number Two: MAN.

10. North American Mammal Mystery

1. Answers will vary. Possible responses: Do spearheads and ax points appear among the fossil bones of the mammals? Does anyone know how many North American mammals were living at the time the humans arrived? **2.** a. mammoth, mastodon, b. cat, c. camel, d. sloth, f. beaver, g. bear, h. horse. **3.** Answers will vary. Possible thoughts: Federal and state programs are in place to restrict hunting endangered species; there's plenty of food to go around; the environment is suitable for survival. **4.** Answers will vary. Possible thoughts: The mammals breed at a high rate, thus keeping the population going; many animals live where humans have a tough time finding them. **5.** Microbe, disease. BRAIN BUILDERS: Challenge Number One: They may have died due to wide-spread disease. Challenge Number Two: They may have died due to "change" in the climate.

11. Fossils on Hold

1. Sketches will vary. A coelacanth tail looks something like this:

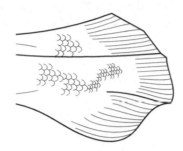

2. AGE OF DINOSAURS   **3.** Ginkgo   **4.** 17. BRAIN BUILDERS:
Challenge Number One: It has to first appear as a prehistoric fossil.
Its species survives for millions of years. Challenge Number Two: Yes.
A fossil is evidence of PAST geologic life.

12. Let's Ban Man

1. cHemical poisoning, overpopUlation, poor Management, increased
poAching, lack of iNterest, overfiShing.   **2.** Students should circle
woolly mammoth (moth-butterfly-like insect), passenger pigeon (pig,
hog, or swine), saber-tooth cat (saber-sharp-edged sword).   **3.** domestic
animals.   **4.** Significant risk means exposed to harm or danger that
could lead to permanent loss or injury. BRAIN BUILDERS: Challenge
Number One: EXIT. Challenge Number Two: END.

Section 2: Early Human Life on Earth

13. New Face from an Old Skull

1. Probably fruit, insects, and worms.   **2.** The skull had small, worn-
down teeth, indicating a diet of soft, easy-to-chew food.   **3.** They may
have decomposed (rotted). Scavengers may have eaten the bones or carried them away.   **4.** (a) teeth, (b) lower jaw, (c) cheek, (d) chin, (e) upper
jaw.   **5.** rib, pelvic, femur, shoulder blade, shin. BRAIN BUILDERS:
Challenge Number One: A mixed-up family tree. Challenge Number Two:
Mr. <u>Tee tho</u>ught, scr<u>ib</u>ble.

14. Who Ate My Kangaroo?

1. Five times: (a) emu, femur, (b) Emu, emulsion, (c) lemur.   **2.** (left
to right) EMU, KOALA BEAR, KANGAROO, PLATYPUS, ANTEATER,
WALLABY (mammals); CROCODILE (reptile); ANT (insect). The nine-
letter word is MIGRATION.   **3.** moose, horse, caribou, bison, sheep.
BRAIN BUILDERS: Challenge Number One: In the letters that spell
menu: e, m, u. Challenge Number Two: Use a pencil to write the word
mammals. Then erase the word. Friction from the eraser caused mammals to disappear.

15. Early Artists Show Their Skill

1. Answers will vary. Scientists may never find enough clues. **2.** a. toe; b. players; c. check; d. name; e. railroad; f. papers. **3.** Sketches will vary. a. Answers will vary. b. Answers will vary. c. Answers will vary. Accept any reasonable answer. **4.** X is 70,000 years old. BRAIN BUILDERS: Challenge Number One: organ – heart; vessel – artery. Challenge Number Two: <u>archae</u>ology.

16. Egyptian Cave Art

1. The experts first saw photos. **2.** To find out if the drawings are real or products of a hoax. **3.** No. It is possible for predynastic rock drawings to be discovered in northern Egypt. **4.** Some may hold fast to certain ideas or theories and may not be tempted to change their minds. **5.** PSEUDO. **6.** Answers will vary. **7.** A wearing away of the art over time. Maybe only a few people were interested in producing "first-rate" art. BRAIN BUILDERS: Challenge Number One: Possible answers: art, soil, tools, cloth, rags, shoes, hoes, logs, trees, grass, clothes, glass, and so on. Challenge Number Two: The animals are rat and cat.

17. Early Man Appears

1. Answers will vary. Scientists, of course, want to conduct further studies to learn all they can about Kennewick Man. Conversely, the Indian population wants Kennewick Man to be reburied and left alone. **2.** atmosphere, stops, dies, decays, replaced, remaining, age. **3.** Probably the teeth. The shape and condition of the teeth should reveal a person's diet. **4.** hyoid, fibula, humerus, scapula, ulna, tibia, thoracic, sternum, patella, skull. BRAIN BUILDERS: Challenge Number One: The second tongue twister: B<u>ob O'Ne</u>ill. Challenge Number Two: It would be backward: <u>Man</u>dible.

18. Keeping the Past Alive

1. a. Too much high water; b. not enough interest; c. too many tourists; d. wild beasts roaming the streets. Message (c) offers the best description. **2.** Plants, sOuvenirs, daMage, Paint, nEglect, vIsitors, ceIlings. **3.** Probably because it's more fun to go on a hunt; it provides a creative challenge to find something new. **4.** rebury. BRAIN BUILDERS: Challenge Number One: a. SUN, b. RUST, c. SLEET. Challenge Number Two:

<u>Volcanic ash and volcanic cinders</u>
Pompeii

Section 3: Getting to Know the Lithosphere

19. Leaving the Lava Behind 1

1. LOOTERS   **2.** Answers will vary.   **3.** Possible answers: Seismologists warn of tremors; faster modes of transportation; better roads and trails for evacuation; more support available from nearby islands; better communication facilities, and so on.   **4.** Melt, Anxious, skY, smOke, warNing. BRAIN BUILDERS: Challenge Number One: In the first letter of VOLCANO turn the V upside down and you'll get a cone shape. Challenge Number Two: PLANTS.

20. Leaving the Lava Behind 2

1. 1. Heavy solid rock exists under extreme pressure.   2. As pressure decreases, rock begins to melt under intense heat.   3. Liquid rock, known as magma, forms deep within the Earth.   4. As more rock melts, magma rises upward.   5. The magma, mixed with steam, moves into the crust. 6. The magma and gases explode from the Earth.   7. Hot gases, lava, and rocks blast into the air.   **2.** First line: doof (food); Second line: retaw (water); Third line: retlehs (shelter); Fourth line: noitatinas (sanitation); Fifth line: gnihtolc (clothing).   **3.** Possible responses: loud noises, rumblings, small earthquakes, slight tremors, shaking, cracks appear in ground, smoke rises from cracks, bulge appears on surface of volcano, ground lifts, buildup and release of gases, appearance of dust, and so forth.   **4.** Product One: GAS or ASH; Product Two: GAS or ASH. **5.** basalt, vapor. BRAIN BUILDER: ba<u>salt</u>.

21. Volcano Secrets

1. Shells and other fossils.   **2.** Use 5 letters in carbon to spell bacon. **3.** The C in VOLCANO appears in the center of the word VOLCANO. The C represents a crater or caldera.   **4.** bulging, ground, carbon dioxide, steam. BRAIN BUILDERS: Challenge Number One: (from top to bottom) DASH, RASH, SASH, BASH, CASH, MASH. Challenge Number Two: About 23 days.

22. Earthquakes 1

1. a. sways, b. rolls, c. shakes or vibrates, d. rumbles, e. trembles **2.** Perhaps the homes are less expensive, they may be well-developed areas, maybe the people think an earthquake won't happen, and so on. **3.** The arrows should connect the letters in the following manner: (c) to (d) to (f) to (a) to (b) to (e).   **4.** 7.9 **5.** Friends, relatives, etc. **6.** Food, clothing, shelter, medical aid, aid in removing the dead and injured, and so on. BRAIN BUILDERS: Challenge Number One: It happens too far underground. Challenge Number Two: In the "ice" part of ep<u>ice</u>nter.

23. Earthquakes 2

1. a. waves, b. soil. The line will show an L-shape. **2.** "Seismo" refers to earthquake activity. **3.** Probably not unless they own property in California or have friends or relatives living there. **4.** Only as an item of interest. People owning property in California or having friends or relatives living there might express concern. **5.** Human-made structures kill many people during a major earthquake. Examples: buildings falling on people, bridges breaking apart and crushing people, flying debris from structures injuring or killing people, and so on. BRAIN BUILDERS: Challenge Number One: seismic waves. Challenge Number Two: Rocks breaking, slipping past each other, sending out energy waves in several directions.

24. Nature's Quake Predictors

1. Sketches will vary. **2.** Descriptions will vary. **3.** a. rodents, b. snakes, c. chickens, d. canines, e. birds. **4.** When or where, when or where, size or magnitude. BRAIN BUILDERS: The letters spell tremors and shakes: t s r e h m a k o r e s s; t s r e h m a k o r e s s.

25. Glacier Alert 1

1. 3,600 days **2.** Almost 23 years old **3.** 34.99 or 35 **4.** Answers will vary for a, b, c, and d. BRAIN BUILDERS: Challenge Number One: The letters CIE unscrambled produce ICE. If you remove these letters from GLACIER, all that will remain of glacier is GLAR. Challenge Number Two: RACE.

26. Glacier Alert 2

1. Hot weather **2.** dirt, silt, wood, tree, stone, rat, bat, and so on. **3.** Possible responses: flood damage to property, plants, and animals; may disrupt people's lives and affect local economy; and so on. **4.** warmer temperature, natural cycle of ice buildup and melting, etc. **5.** forests, agriculture. **6.** humans, knife, animals. BRAIN BUILDERS: Challenge Number One: bird. Challenge Number Two: Because Maria meant to say "gravity."

27. Inner Space Travel

1. Limestone, dolomite **2.** caverns **3.** Sketches will vary. Stalactites should appear on the roof of the cave and stalagmites should be on the floor of the cave directly below the stalactites. **4.** Strategies for remembering will vary. **5.** Sketches will vary. **6.** Possible responses: Don't leave any litter behind; Don't touch any of the cave structures; Don't take any souvenirs; and so on. BRAIN BUILDER: Add "rn" to cave for cavern, a large cave.

28. Mapping in Outer and Inner Space

1. a. The direction-giving would be totally confusing. b. The person receiving directions would have difficulty knowing where to go. **2.** a. They might experience new discoveries. b. They might gather information needed for future study. **3.** Answers will vary. **4.** Aviators: Help pilots avoid crashing into mountain peaks. Scientists: Help them study drainage patterns in valleys. Defense Department: Help Defense Department guide missiles with accuracy. **5.** Answers will vary. BRAIN BUILDER: Arrange the letters in map to read amp. Amp is the abbreviation for amperage. An ampere is the standard unit for measuring the strength of an electric current.

29. Global Positioning System

1. Tanks, soldiers, shelters, convoys. **2.** Answers will vary. Possible responses: volcanic disturbances, landslide movement, tsunamis buildup, glacier movement, animal migration, and so forth. **3.** receiver, a. rice, b. veer. **4.** a. GPS could map out the trail and show curves, obstructions, etc. b. GPS could fix the position with accuracy. c. GPS would put the boat within yards of the fishing spot. BRAIN BUILDERS: Use the letters s, i, g, n, a, l from Global Positioning System.

Section 4: Listening to the Environment

30. Chromium 6 on Trial

1. Two. Mr. Crawford, Mr. Crawford. In a two-lettered chemical symbol the first letter is always capitalized. **2.** From the industrial plants using chromium in their operation. **3.** How much Chromium 6 in the water is too much? **4.** The word in GROUND is poison. The word in WATER is contamination. BRAIN BUILDERS: Challenge Number One: Cr six. Challenge Number Two: chum.

31. Mercury Menace

1. The Hg is the chemical symbol for mercury. **2.** a. anemia, b. tremors, c. deformities, d. paralysis. **3.** Answers will vary. **4.** Seven ounces per week equals 22.8 pounds per year. 364 ounces divided by 12 months per year equals 22.75 pounds, rounded off equals 22.8 pounds per year. Kathleen is eating fish slightly over the suggested limit. BRAIN BUILDERS: Challenge Number One: quicksilver. Challenge Number Two: As a planet, as an automobile, and as a name for a Greek god.

32. Global Warming Warning 1

1. Natural gas, coal, and oil. **2.** 3.7 + 2.8 + 3.2 + 3.4 + 2.4 = 15.5; 15.5 divided by 5 = 3.1 or 3.1 percent. **3.** The numbers in order complete the answers: a. An increase in violent storms. b. A melting of polar ice caps. c. Rising sea levels. **4.** Scientists receive information on global warming from computer climate models and weather satellite data. BRAIN BUILDERS: Challenge Number One: Rearrange the letters in coal to spell cola, a soft drink. Challenge Number Two: One half of carbon is "car." A car produces carbon as an exhaust product.

33. Global Warming Warning 2

1. USA. All five words carry the letters "USA." **2.** greenhouse gas. **3.** Possible answers: C—coastal flooding, carbon dioxide increase, crop failure. L—loss of certain vegetation, longer dry seasons, loss of water. I—invasion of certain plants, islands become submerged, ice (glaciers) melt. M—much of the wildlife disappears, melting of polar ice cap. A—atmospheric problems continue, anxiety builds in people. T—trouble for fishing industry, farming communities and forestry programs; temperature rises. E—ecosystems become weak and unstable, economic problems would arise. **4.** Answers will vary. BRAIN BUILDERS: Challenge Number One: In the "dust" part of in<u>dust</u>rial. Challenge Number Two: Calm.

34. Ocean Currents and Weather

1. STORMS. **2.** a. record rainfall in California; b. tornadoes in the Southeast; c. flooding in the Southeast; d. flooding in Peru; e. droughts in Indonesia. **3.** They would have a tough time making predictions of future weather. **4.** Recently La Niña has been blamed for causing "drought from the Great Plains to the Southeast." **5.** Sketches will vary. **6.** The pelican's preferred meal is an anchovy. BRAIN BUILDERS: Challenge Number One: Moisture in the atmosphere. Challenge Number Two: NaCl, sodium chloride, is salt. You would find salt in salinity by combining the letters s, a, l, and t.

35. Pollution Problem

1. Pollution will increase through added use of resources. As the population increases, more waste will be produced. **2.** By exploding ash, extensive lava flows, developing mud flows, smoke from burning forests and buildings, and so on. **3.** Extensive fires, broken gas lines, ruptured water and sewer pipes. **4.** Pollen, Ash, sooT, dIrt, dUst, gAses, smokE, aeroSol. **5.** Moving air. **6.** Satellite images. BRAIN BUILDERS: Challenge Number One: <u>precipitation</u>. Challenge Number Two: NEON.

36. Pollution Solution

1. It's cheaper to burn coal, gas, and oil than get power from the sun. **2.** Photovoltaic cells. **3.** By using solar power, no pollution particles will be produced. **4.** Answers will vary. **5.** 30 percent. **6.** According to engineers, cars powered by gasoline and other fossil fuels will always emit some amount of smog-forming material. BRAIN BUILDERS: Challenge Number One: An ant. "Ant" makes up three letters out of the ten letters needed to spell pollutants (or 30 percent). Challenge Number Two: HYDROCARBONS.

37. Forever Organisms

1. Answers will vary. Students might respond with "People need to really care," "People need to realize how serious the situation is," and so on. **2.** a. poachers; b. loggers; c. wars, nations; d. dams; e. mining; f. cattle grazing; g. overpopulation, supply; h. pollution, toxic, materials. **3.** The illustration shows $5 billion over the next 10 years. a. $200,000,000. Divide 25 into $5 billion. b. $20,000,000. Divide 10 into $200 million. **4.** a. Brazil, b. California, c. Caribbean, d. Chile, e. China, f. Congo, g. Mediterranean, h. Philippines. BRAIN BUILDERS: Challenge Number One: Draw a circle. Write the words ANIMALS and PLANTS around the circle. The circle represents the world. Challenge Number Two: Draw an eight-sided shape (stop sign) and write "extinction" inside of the shape.

Section 5: Ocean Features and Related Creatures

38. Save the Coral

1. a. eel, b. crab, c. algae, d. sponge, e. fish, f. shrimp. **2.** global warming, rise. **3.** (left to right) VERTICAL: rubbish, sewage, trash. (top to bottom) HORIZONTAL: garbage, toxins, chemicals. **4.** Answers will vary. BRAIN BUILDERS: Challenge Number One: By removing the letter R. Without the R the word becomes COAL, a black, combustible mineral. Challenge Number Two: Place another letter R next to the R in CORAL to make it CORRAL, a pen for holding horses.

39. Lost City Found

1. Sketches will vary. **2.** 10 spires. **3.** Ms. Alc spelled backwards is clams; Ms. Row spelled backwards (with rearrangement) is worms. The sea creatures are clams and worms. **4.** The data provides fresh information for observation and study. The research adds data to the knowledge bank. **5.** It means there are many things yet to be discovered by humans. The vast ocean depths make a safe environment for yet-to-be discovered organisms. BRAIN BUILDERS: Challenge Number One: The chemical symbol for sulfur is S; the letters that spell the common name for Fe is IRON. Challenge Number Two: The letters spelling HEAT make up 56 percent of the letters needed to spell thermal. Challenge Number Three: clam, crab, and worm.

40. Island Under Water

1. Possible answer: Perhaps landform features known to be associated with islands scattered around the world. **2.** Melting ice sheets caused the sea level to rise. **3.** Answers will vary. Global warming could cause polar ice to melt and cause a rise in sea level. **4.** They could do whatever is necessary to reduce the greenhouse effect. **5.** a. buffalo, b. saber-tooth cat, c. camel, d. mammoth. BRAIN BUILDERS: Challenge Number One: Since you may use the same letter once, you can only get one spelling of island. Challenge Number Two: snail.

41. Don't Go Near the Water

1. a. ocean bacteria, b. "You are really tan." **2.** Answers will vary. Perhaps lifeguards or security personnel should be responsible for making sure everyone understands the problem. They should not let anyone enter the water while the area remains risky. **3.** Possible answers: R—rubbish, raw sewage. U—utensils, underbrush, urine. N—nutrients, nitrates, nondairy products. O—oil, organic waste matter. F—food particles, fertilizer, factory wastes. F—fruit peelings, foliage, fish, fowl. **4.** Possible answers: Cite people who leave rubbish near curb gutters, cite people who wash oil and chemicals into the drain, keep people posted on the problem and offer guidelines for reducing pollution, continue monitoring the areas known to produce excessive pollution. BRAIN BUILDERS: Challenge Number One: Move the letters around in "for fun" to spell "runoff." Challenge Number Two: Remove the letter s.

42. Fate of the Fish

1. Answers to both will vary. **2.** "Protect our resources." **3.** a. at risk, endangered; b. Probably all three terms apply. More reports would be needed to determine if the pollock have disappeared. **4.** a. ocean perch, b. sawfish, c. halibut, d. giant sea bass, e. whale shark. **5.** Answers will vary. Restrictions have been placed on longline fishing until more data is gathered. BRAIN BUILDERS: Challenge Number One: FINS. Challenge Number Two: He could tell by the "scales" on the fish. Challenge Number Three: fi*she*rman (she), fish*her*man (her).

43. Microbes from Across the Sea

1. Mammals: bat, bear, cat; rodent: rat. **2.** Mammals: man, ram; mollusk—snail; insect—ant. **3.** a. 10½, b. 110, c. 171, d. 200. In some areas state or federal regulations require a vessel to dump ballast water 200 miles out to sea. **4.** To prevent the spread of harmful microorganisms. **5.** Circle the letters that spell jellyfish in Row 1. Circle the letters that spell mussels in Row 2. Circle the letters that spell clams in Row 3. Sea creature #1: jellyfish; Sea creature #2: mussels; Sea creature #3: clams. **6.** Answers will vary. BRAIN BUILDERS: Challenge Number One: It has an "organ" in name only: micro*organ*ism. Microorganisms do not have organs. Challenge Number Two: Accept any logical answer.

44. Cormorants Under Siege

1. catfish, trout, salmon, bass.   **2.** Strict regulations on shooting cormorants, pollution cleanup, ban on pesticides.   **3.** 174 days.
4. Possible answers: Some birds may eat more than a pound of fish a day; some of the fish may die and decompose before the birds eat them; the cormorants would have a hard time eating all of the trout; some of the trout would escape; a few trout may grow too big to eat; and so on.
5. Answers will vary.   **6.** Fishermen tie a ring around the cormorant's neck. BRAIN BUILDERS: Challenge Number One: (possible answers):

c o r m f i s h o r a n t

c o r f m i o s r h a n t

Challenge Number Two: There is a cormorant overpopulation. (cormorant over population)

45. The No-Wimp Shrimp

1. a. crab, b. shrimp, c. snail, d. fish.   **2.** a. canal, b. ribs. The two splash zone organisms are a snail and a crab.   **3.** Sometimes solutions to problems cause more problems. Student answers will vary.   **4.** Answers will vary.   **5.** fast, last. BRAIN BUILDERS: Challenge Number One: IMP. Challenge Number Two: ANT.

46. Jellyfish on the Rocks

1. The body of a jellyfish has NO BONES. A jellyfish has SOFT BODY PARTS.   **2.** SAND   **3.** shape, size.   **4.** Jellyfish show little change over millions of years, ocean conditions today are similar to those millions of years ago, and so on. BRAIN BUILDERS: Challenge Number One: OCEAN, SEA. Challenge Number Two: EEL, CORAL. Challenge Number Three: TERN, LOON.

47. Anemone by the Sea

1. *Finding Nemo*.   **2.** nematocysts.   **3.** nerve cells.   **4.** stArfish, teNtacles, tidE, pools, sMall fish, bOdy shape, oNe, invErtebrate. BRAIN BUILDERS: Challenge Number One: PHEnomenal. Challenge Number Two: The illustration should show power balancing over a pointed triangular shape. The line represents the balancing stick.

48. Squid Freak from Down Deep

1. There are 5,280 feet in a mile. The creatures swim anywhere between 1.14 and 2.84 miles (one to three miles).   **2.** Scientists didn't have the needed equipment to discover new species.   **3.** a. bat, wings; b. base; c. creature's, arms, thin, end; d. bent; e. eighty.   **4.** 23 feet.   **5.** Circle (d). Calamari is inside the squid. Calamari is the squid cooked as food. BRAIN BUILDERS: Challenge Number One: It shows sea mammals, fish, and bird eating squid. Also, it indicates squid eating fish. Challenge Number Two: INK.

49. Stingless Stingrays

1. barb.   **2.** Answers will vary.   **3.** Possible responses: Some people like the challenge; others may plan to enter the water.   **4.** Most students would agree that removing the barbs limits the stingray's defense mechanism. They need their whip-like tails with stingers to ward off enemies.   **5.** The enemy is the coastal shark.   **6.** Squid, shrimp, sardine, crab, clam, oyster. BRAIN BUILDERS: Challenge Number One: Sn is the chemical symbol for tin. The symbol is number 50 on the periodic table. Arrange the words and letters like this: Sn = tin, S + tingray. Challenge Number Two: Rearrange the letters in "tiny rags" to spell stingray.

50. Plight of the Sturgeon

1. a. pollution, b. overfishing, c. poaching.   **2.** pounds, cured, salt, cans, jars.   **3.** Sturgeon eggs prepared for the consumer are known as caviar.   **4.** $900 \times 35.5 = \$31,950$.   **5.** Poachers continue to defy the law for the large sums of money they receive from selling sturgeon eggs.   **6.** Answers will vary. A ban might help save the declining fish population. Some say a ban will only increase poaching.   **7.** There are several possible answers: Ban the sale of beluga eggs, increase law enforcement to stop poaching, try to convince people to stop eating caviar, and so forth. BRAIN BUILDERS: Challenge Number One: Rearrange the letters to spell roe, fish eggs. Challenge Number Two: Fish eggs in salt (NaCl is the chemical formula for salt.)

51. Predator Challenge

1. Possible answers: P—perch, pelican, porpoise, puffin. R—red fish, rockfish. E—eel, egret, elephant seal. D—dogfish, dolphin, devilfish. A—anemone, albatross, angel fish. T—turtle, tern, thrasher shark. O—octopus, otter, osprey. R—rock bass, rooster fish.   **2.** Possible answers: P—parrot, polar bear, panther. R—rattlesnake, raccoon. E—eagle, egret. D—dragonfly, daddy longlegs. A—alligator, anteater, African lion, albatross. T—tiger, turtle. O—ocelot, opossum, oyster catcher. R—raptor, robin.   **3.** (any order) alligator, shark, bear, and cougar.   **4.** The predator is an alligator.   **5.** Answers will vary. Killing animals won't solve the problem. A better solution might be to solve the world population problem.   **6.** Answers will vary. Perhaps people should spend less time in the water or heed warnings. Again, as the population continues to climb, more attacks can be expected. BRAIN BUILDERS: Challenge Number One: rodent: RAT; a female deer: DOE; large extinct bird: DODO. Challenge Number Two: PREY.

52. The Sea Otter's Dilemma

1. Orca.   **2.** Answers will vary.   **3.** Answers will vary. Possible response: Sea otters and people compete for the same food.   **4.** a. parasite, b. bacteria, c. boat, d. shark.   **5.** Answers will vary. BRAIN BUILDERS: Challenge Number One: mammal. Challenge Number Two: H_2O.

53. Sea Lions Take Charge

1. Great White Shark. **2.** The sea lion may not be afraid of loud sounds. A sea lion's hunger may be stronger than loud noises. **3.** Answers will vary. **4.** Responses will vary. Few fishermen would feel sorry for the sea lion. **5.** Answers will vary. **6.** Environmentalist: P—proud, puzzled. E—enjoyment, emotional. S—serene, sympathetic. T—talkative, trembly. Angler: P—put out, pugnacious. E—emotional, enraged. S—scornful, self-pity. T—ticked-off, terrible. **7.** They should seek a solution that would satisfy the majority of people. Also, they should develop an effective nonlethal means to chase off sea lions. BRAIN BUILDERS: Challenge Number One: Use the first four letters in sea lion to spell seal. Challenge Number Two: SNAIL.

54. A Whale of a Tale

1. amino, lenses, eyes. **2.** Around 105+ years old. **3.** Water, Harpoon, cAlf, mammaL, blubbEr, Spout. **4.** a. 92 to 128 years old; b. 126 to 174 years old. BRAIN BUILDERS: Challenge Number One: In the ton part of the word: plank<u>ton</u>. A ton equals 2,000 pounds. Challenge Number Two: 70 feet.

Section 6: What's Happening in Space?

55. Taking on the Universe

1. a. 7, b. 3, c. 6, d. 5, e. 10, f. 9, g. 2, h. 1, i. 4, j. 8. **2.** a. 9, b. 16, c. 8, d. 20, e. 15. **3.** Answers will vary. Scientists are dealing with a theory. According to the theory, the event took place 12 to 20 billion years ago. **4.** Answers will vary. **5.** Answers will vary. BRAIN BUILDERS: Challenge Number One: EARTH, SATURN, and PLUTO. Challenge Number Two:

56. New Planets in Town

1. wobble, gravity. **2.** A little over eight minutes. **3.** brown dwarfs. **4.** cliffs, rocks, dust, plains. **5.** Each time a new planet is discovered, it raises the possibility that more will be found in the future. **6.** Yes. Mostly because a star with a long life gives a nearby planet more time for life to evolve. BRAIN BUILDERS: Challenge Number One: PLANT, ANIMAL. Challenge Number Two: e, a, r, t, h.

57. Mars: A Watery World?

1. erosion, water.   **2.** polar ice caps, reservoirs under the surface.
3. Letter g appears three times. There are three spellings of hydrogen.
4. pockets, water.   **5.** Probably in hopes of making new discoveries
that might lead to future colonization. BRAIN BUILDERS: Challenge
Number One: RED PLANET. Challenge Number Two: SWARM.
Challenge Number Three: SCRAM.

58. Asteroid Probes Coming Up

1. composition, shape, size.   **2.** asteroid, Earth, collide, reptiles, vanish.
3. plAnetoid, teleScope, Tiny, bElt, oRbit, thOusands, axIs, Diameter.
4. Perhaps its composition might reveal important information; its
atmosphere, temperature, orbital path, and so on, might be helpful.
BRAIN BUILDERS: Challenge Number One: O as R te B ro I id T.
Challenge Number Two: STAR.

59. Eros: Space Mountain Asteroid

1. Sketches will vary. Most drawings will be oblong. Features may
include a groove, boulders, a rocky surface, and craters.   **2.** primitive,
solar system.   **3.** Eros would sink. It has a higher density than water.
4. 8.4 grams per cubic centimeter.   **5.** Answers will vary. Perhaps
there may be forms of life on them too.   **6.** Answers will vary. BRAIN
BUILDERS: Challenge Number One: ORES. Challenge Number Two:
Write the word ASTEROIDS, then cross out letters A, S, T, I, and D.

60. Paranoid Rhymes with Asteroid

1. Science fiction films, doomsday stories, traumatic news reports make
believers out of them.   **2.** a. Drawings will vary. b. The Earth and the
asteroid must meet at the same time.   **3.** Tsunamis. *Tsunami* is the
Japanese word for "tidal wave."   **4.** Pieces may land in the desert;
numerous fragments hit the ocean and sink.   **5.** Take it to an expert in
the field. BRAIN BUILDERS: Challenge Number One: ASTER. Challenge
Number Two: Remove the "a" from asteroid to get the chemical, steroid.
Challenge Number Three: RAT, TOAD, and DOE.

61. Twenty-Two and Counting

1. frozen (6), water (5), rocky (5), matter (6).   **2.** Top line: valleys;
middle line: mountains; bottom line: craters, volcanoes.   **3.** Amount,
reflected light.   **4.** It might indicate something about the planet's composition. BRAIN BUILDERS: Challenge Number One: SUN, STAR.
Challenge Number Two: All letters combine to spell SATELLITE.

62. The Moons of Jupiter

1. Sketches will vary.   **2.** a. Answers will vary. It would depend on several
factors: temperature, salinity of the water, and so forth. b. Sketches will

vary.   **3.** sulfur.   **4.** magnetic field.   **5.** To find out under what conditions life can exist. BRAIN BUILDERS: Challenge Number One: FROZEN H (two) O or FROZEN HOH. Challenge Number Two: Europe should be Europa and cork should be rock. Challenge Number Three: Ohio or Iowa, lion, and Iodine and Niobium.

63. Meteor Trails and Comet Tales

1. high speed, heat.   **2.** Fireball.   **3.** 3.6 meteors per second.
4. Possible response: Ideal conditions for viewing a meteor shower would include the following: a clear sky with no moon visible, fair weather conditions, and a viewing point several miles away from city lights.   **5.** about 37.3 million miles.   **6.** Recent reports show some comets contain large amounts of solid matter. BRAIN BUILDERS: Challenge Number One: From the letters c, o, m, e, t, found in the words in the phrase. Challenge Number Two: cometeor

64. Meteorite Mysteries

1. fragMent, Earth, sTony, nickEl, theOry, iRon, scientIst, craTer, fiEld.
2. The data would suggest that the solar system and the meteors originated at about the same time.   **3.** Perhaps the meteorite originated from space material found "among the stars."   **4.** To preserve the elements contained in the meteorite.   **5.** asteroid, asteroids.   **6.** It could if all data are accurate. One theory holds that an asteroid could have smashed into Mars and sent pieces flying into space. A fragment may have eventually become trapped in the Earth's gravitational field. BRAIN BUILDERS: Challenge Number One: TREE. Challenge Number Two: PLANET, STAR, SATELLITE.

65. From Stars to Galaxies

1. 9 zeros.   **2.** Scientists can't be sure. A gap of 10 billion years leaves a large "safety margin."   **3.** 6.5 billion light-years.   **4.** Possible response: A star collapses. It becomes dense and gravity increases. Light cannot escape.   **5.** motion, stars, gas. BRAIN BUILDERS: Challenge Number One: Stars, moon, Mars, meteor, meteorite, satellite. Challenge Number Two: Bob lacks . . . . wholesome . . . .

66. Telescopes and Beyond

ACROSS: 3. stars   4. comets   6. asteroids.   **DOWN:** 1. planets
2. meteors   5. moon.   **2.** A more powerful telescope increases the chances of discovering new objects in space.   **3.** Answers will vary.
4. They should be protected with insulated clothes and strong surrounding structures.   **5.** Answers will vary. BRAIN BUILDERS: Challenge Number One: SEE. Challenge Number Two: NEPTUNE.

Section 7: Life on Land and Water

67. As the Worm Turns

1. They stay alive and continue to grow by absorbing energy from the chemicals that seep through cracks in the ocean floor. **2.** By living in deep water, these worms do without light, without food, without movement, and without stress (as we know it). **3.** Sixteen ounces in a pound plus 360 degrees in a circle (figure round) equals 376. Subtract 358 from 376 and you'll get 18. The giant earthworm was 18 inches long. **4.** Answers will vary. The specialist needs to find out what the earthworm's internal organs look like to determine its species status. **5.** a. Tapeworm, b. Fluke, c. Ascaris, d. Trichina. BRAIN BUILDERS: Challenge Number One: luck. Challenge Number Two: The two o's in the word roundworm.

68. It's All About Ants

1. a. wasps, bees; b. social; c. legs; d. head, thorax, and abdomen. **2.** PEST. **3.** DECAPITATE. **4.** The population should grow since the ants aren't fighting and killing each other. **5.** Answers will vary. No one knows for sure. BRAIN BUILDERS: Challenge Number One: Write the word ants six times in a wavelike pattern. Challenge Number Two: ANTIQUE. Challenge Number Three: GIANT.

69. Insects Two

1. Grasshopper sketches will vary. **2.** Chewing. **3.** To communicate with other insects. **4.** The flying heroes were GULLS. **5.** They said there were no reports on the damage poisoning might have on other animals in the environment. Responses will vary. **6.** 1,500 × 38 = 57,000. 57,000 divided by 2,000 equals 28.5 tons. BRAIN BUILDERS: Challenge Number One: COMET, METEOR, ROCKET. Challenge Number Two: GRASS, ROOTS.

70. Where Have All the Froggies Gone? 1

1. moist, source. **2.** a. loss of land; b. new predators; c. fertilizers; d. pesticides; e. pollutants. **3.** Answers will vary. **4.** They set aside land for the protection of the toad. **5.** a. pan; b. map; c. ham; d. bin; e. aim; f. bam; g. bib; h. nab. BRAIN BUILDERS: Challenge Number One: POPUL (or ATION). Challenge Number Two: Shanika wrote amphibian on a piece of paper, then she circled the two "i"s. "The letter i," she said, "cannot see."

71. Where Have All the Froggies Gone? 2

1. a. Need, experience, their; b. protection, develop; c. involve, people, wants, blamed, species. **2.** Answers will vary. **3.** a. blood, b. bones, c. eyes, d. head, e. muscles, f. nerves, g. skin, h. tongue. **4.** Tree, Ohio, Oregon, Aqueduct, Dirt. BRAIN BUILDERS: Challenge Number One: A tadpole. Challenge Number Two: Salamander. Challenge Number three: . . . . do to advance . . . .

72. The California Condor Comeback 1

1. 94 percent   **2.** 86 percent; answers will vary.   **3.** RAPTURE.
4. Canine, cAt, Rabbit, Rat, bIrd, Owl, sNake. BRAIN BUILDERS:
Challenge Number One: M–EAT MEAT. Challenge Number Two: COON.

73. The California Condor Comeback 2

1. bullets, hunters.   **2.** around $296,000.   **3.** To save it from extinction.
It needs to be part of an ecological system.   **4.** PROTECTION.   **5.** Probably because they don't want to be blamed for the drop in California Condor population.   **6.** immune.   **7.** If lead poisoning continues to kill condors, their best chance of survival would be to remain in captivity. BRAIN BUILDERS: Challenge Number One: CA CONDOR. (CA is the postal abbreviation for California.) Challenge Number Two: PITY.

74. Rodent Roundup 1

1. incisoRs, crOps, Disease, Ears or Eyes, gNawing, planTs.   **2.** gnawing, incisors, ears or eyes, plants, crops, disease.   **3.** grease.   **4.** city officials, rodent experts, health people—anyone who can help solve the problem.
5. Answers will vary. BRAIN BUILDERS: Challenge Number One: gnawing rodents: BEAVER, RAT; two mammals: BAT, BEAR; insect: BEE. Challenge Number Two: a picture of a mouse.

75. Rodent Roundup 2

1. Mild winter, construction, new homes.   **2.** Answers will vary. People who find voles invading their homes will probably answer "yes."   **3.** If there are laws against firing weapons within the city limits, then people would be lawbreakers. Stray bullets could hit houses, people, etc. Also, pet cats and dogs could eat the vole poison.   **4.** Answers will vary. People who move into an area need to buy a home. They should expect some problems to arise.   **5.** Probably not. Most people want the problem solved immediately before much damage is done.   **6.** 9,600 voles.
7. 3; 2 voles; 1 meadow mouse (vole). BRAIN BUILDERS: Challenge Number One: LOVE. Challenge Number Two: TRAP.

76. The Smallest of Critters

1. reptiLes, sEed, frUit, biRds.   **2.** 969 paper clips.   **3.** Possible answers: Too many predators, disease, climate change, food shortage.   **4.** It would help prevent the extinction of the species.   **5.** Fossils, million, tiny, animals, scientists, groups. BRAIN BUILDERS: Challenge Number One: pack animal: MULE; Australian bird—EMU; snakelike fish—EEL. Challenge Number Two: APE. Challenge Number Three: EndANGER, dANGER.

Section 8: What's Up in Genetic Science?

77. Genetic Review

Matching: 1. strand **2.** trait **3.** DNA **4.** mutation **5.** clone **6.** gene **7.** progeria **8.** encode **9.** cell **10.** embryo **11.** transplant **12.** stem cell **13.** gene map **14.** variation **15.** gene splicing **16.** genomics **17.** chromosome **18.** genome **19.** genetic code **20.** gene therapy. BRAIN BUILDERS: Challenge Number One: RED (the color). Challenge Number Two: twin, twin.

78. From One Gene to Another 1

1. Possible answers: eye color, blood type, skin color, body shape, facial features, genetic disorders, size and shape of organs, etc. **2.** identical **3.** diabetes, obesity **4.** Monkeys are close relatives to humans. By using monkeys, scientists believe they have a better chance to isolate and treat certain diseases. **5.** More tests need to be conducted to check the safety and reliability of the product. BRAIN BUILDERS: Challenge Number One: INSECTS. Challenge Number Two: DEER.

79. From One Gene to Another 2

1. rOdent, fRuit fly, Guinea pig, cAt, moNkey, pIg, Sheep, huMan. **2.** hearing loss, diabetes, obesity, Parkinson's. **3.** Progeria. **4.** Very important. If one person can be helped, then it's worth the effort. **5.** chemicals, drugs. BRAIN BUILDERS: Challenge Number One: A gene mutation. Challenge Number Two: HORSE, MOOSE.

80. Designer Catfish

1. Canals, rivers, breathe, native, mistake. **2.** They didn't expect any problems. However, people should fully understand what an organism needs in its natural habitat before being brought into a new environment. **3.** Answers will vary. Scientists say many people benefit from altered food. **4.** Grow faster. **5.** They might eat the native fish, they could eat plants and other organisms needed to sustain the environment, and so on. BRAIN BUILDERS: Challenge Number One: Take away the letter G. Place RGE between the ET to turn GENETIC into ENERGETIC. Challenge Number Two: Replace the letter T with the letter R to turn GENETIC into GENERIC.

81. Biotech Foods

1. Fruits, vegetables, wheat. **2. ACROSS:** 2. alter 4. corn 5. seeds. **DOWN:** 1. herbicide 4. biotech. **3.** Answers will vary. **4.** When they refuse to obey police orders, when their actions threaten the safety of others, and so on. **5.** Answers will vary. BRAIN BUILDERS: Challenge Number One: CORN. Challenge Number Two: Possible responses: dese, sdee, esde, and so forth.

82. Human Stem Cells

1. a. cardiac, b. cornea, c. pancreas, d. muscle, e. cartilage, f. liver, g. brain, h. cutaneous. **2.** Answers will vary. **3.** Opinions will vary for Items (a) through (e). BRAIN BUILDERS: Challenge Number One: em<u>bryo</u>: Combine these letters to spell boy. Challenge Number Two: MUSCLE.

83. Human Genome

1. a. medical, major; b. treatments, ailments; c. prevent. **2.** Our ability to think and reason at a high level; how we are influenced by our environment. **3.** 90,000. **4.** Answers will vary. **5.** growth, life, reproduction, diseases, and death. BRAIN BUILDERS: Challenge Number One: By arranging the letters in genome to spell "one gem." Challenge Number Two: DNA makes up 100 percent of Dan's name. DNA makes up only three letters or 75 percent of Edna's name.

84. What About Cloning?

1. The drawings should look like their parents. **2.** To coax cells into dividing and producing an organism. **3.** Answers will vary. **4.** CRICKET, BEETLE, MOTH, ANT, HONEYBEE. **5.** Human cloning may never be approved. However, if scientists perfect their procedure and produce healthy animals, more people are likely to accept some phases of human cloning. BRAIN BUILDERS: Challenge Number One: DOE (female deer). Challenge Number Two: NO.

Section 9: Timely Real-Life Topics of Concern

Activities 85 through 91 offer students an opportunity to read and think about real-life topics of concern. They can express their thoughts by writing comments or suggestions for each of the issues. Student responses will vary in this section.

Answer Key for Riddles for the Asking

1. You look well-preserved for a girl your age.
2. In fossil beds or sedimentary beds.
3. Some become petrified with the idea.
4. A fossil.
5. Long time no "sea."
6. Spearmint.
7. Dead.
8. To get to where they were going.
9. Club sandwich.
10. Club Club.
11. A blastoff.
12. Seismic belts.
13. The quake part.
14. They shake on it.
15. The O in rock.
16. They tend to lose their focus.
17. At Epicenters.
18. Cinder (Cinderella).
19. He wanted to stop global warming.
20. In the rough part—dROUGHt.
21. He wanted to experience the greenhouse effect firsthand.
22. It makes up one-third of pollut<u>ant</u>.
23. Because they drift from place to place.
24. Because it had no spine.
25. They go to the CALFeteria.

26. The coral group.

27. Because they're always "lion."

28. Just toss it to him.

29. In Hollywood, California.

30. A GALAxy.

31. An ITE at the end of its name.

32. The letter O.

33. The MOOn.

34. Prey.

35. He was allowed one "carrion."

36. They warn each other by going "caw, caw (car, car)."

37. In the word CAN'T.

38. The emu part—lEMUr.

39. The man part—salaMANder.

40. The fish part—catFISH.

41. Fish cat.

42. They wanted him to become a geneticist.

43. A chromosome.

44. An inherited trait.

45. The number one—clONE.

Other Books of Interest

Science Puzzlers!
150 Ready-to-Use Activities to Make
Learning Fun, Grades 4–8

Robert G. Hoehn

Paperback / 272 pages / 2002
ISBN: 0-7879-6660-6

For the upper elementary and middle school teacher, this unique resource offers 150 science puzzle activities ranging from word scrambles, word searches and categorizing, to variations on crosswords and mini-problem solvers to help you add challenge and humor to instruction while keeping lessons moving at a steady pace. Printed in a lay-flat paper format for easy photocopying, organized into three science areas, and followed by complete answer keys, this indispensable resource gives you an array of lighthearted lessons that will enlighten and motivate your students.

Other Books of Interest

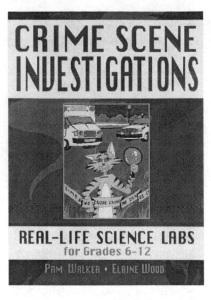

Crime Scene Investigations:
Real-Life Science Labs for Grades 6–12

Pam Walker and Elaine Wood

Paperback / 288 pages / 2002
ISBN: 0-7879-6630-4

Turn your students into super sleuths with the 60 exciting lessons and worksheets this unique resource has to offer! All provide complete teacher background information and activity sheets that challenge students to observe carefully, organize and record data, think critically, and conduct simple tests to solve crimes ranging from theft and vandalism to water pollution. Whatever your training or experience in teaching science, *Crime Scene Investigations* can be an intriguing supplement to instruction. You'll find your students will be eager to learn science concepts and solve a mystery at the same time!

- Reinforce skills of observation, experimentation, and logical thinking.

- Help students identify unknown substances, recognize patterns, and determine the chain of events.

- Demonstrate how reconstruction of past events can influence the outcome of a criminal investigation . . . and more!

Pam Walker (B.S., M.Ed., Ed.S.) has been a teacher since 1981 and has taught science, biology, applied biology/chemistry, physics, health and physical education in grades 9–12.

Elaine Wood (A.B., M.S., Ed.S) has more than 14 years of teaching experience in physical science, biology, chemistry, physics, and applied biology/chemistry in grades 7–12 and has conducted research in genetic engineering.

Ms. Walker and Ms. Wood teach science at Alexander High School in Douglassville, Georgia.

Other Books of Interest

Algebra Out Loud: Learning Mathematics Through Reading and Writing Activities

Pat Mower, Ph.D.

Paperback / 256 pages / 2003
ISBN: 0-7879-6898-6

Algebra Out Loud is a unique resource designed for mathematics instructors who are teaching Algebra I and II. This easy-to-use resource is filled with illustrative examples, strategies, activities, and lessons that will help students more easily understand mathematical text and learn the skills they need to effectively communicate mathematical concepts.

Algebra Out Loud's strategies and activities will give students the edge in learning how to summarize, analyze, present, utilize, and retain mathematical content. The book offers proven writing activities that will engage the students in writing about algebraic vocabulary, processes, theorems, definitions, and graphs. *Algebra Out Loud* gives teachers the tools they need to help their students learn how to communicate about math ideas between student and teacher, student and peers, and student and the wider world.

For quick access and easy use, the activities are printed in a big 8½" x 11" format for photocopying and are organized into eight chapters.

Pat Mower is an associate professor in the Department of Mathematics and Statistics at Washburn University in Topeka, Kansas. Dr. Mower prepares preservice teachers to teach mathematics in elementary, middle, and secondary schools. Her interests include reading and writing in mathematics, and alternative methods for the teaching and learning of mathematics.

Other Books of Interest

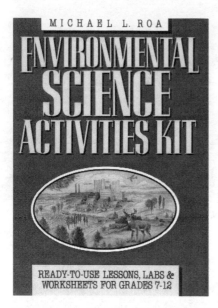

Environmental Science Activities Kit: Ready-to-Use Lessons, Labs, and Worksheets for Grades 7–12

Michael L. Roa

Paperback / 352 pages / 2002
ISBN: 0-7879-6700-9

For earth, life, and physical science teachers, grades 7–12. Included are 32 detailed, interdisciplinary science lessons with complete directions for use and reproducible student activity guide and worksheets, all conveniently organized into six topical units focusing on major environmental issues:

Unit 1: Land Use Issues

Unit 2: Wildlife Issues

Unit 3: Water Issues

Unit 4: Atmospheric Issues

Unit 5: Energy Issues

Unit 6: Human Issues

For easy use, every lesson is completely planned, including a brief summary, suggestions for introduction, list of materials required, teacher preparation and safety considerations, step-by-step teaching directions, questions for discussion, and extensions for further study.

Moreover, four special appendices at the end of the Kit present the names and addresses of governmental agencies and selected organizations concerned with environmental issues plus practical letter-writing suggestions on "How to write for information" and "How to write a letter to a governmental office."

Michael L. Roa has been a teacher since 1969 and has taught grades 4–12 as well as workshops for preservice and inservice teachers. He is the coauthor (with Donnell Tinkelenberg) of *Biology Teacher's Instant Vocabulary Kit* (The Center for Applied Research in Education, 1991).

Other Books of Interest

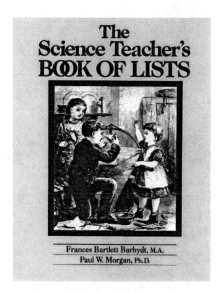

The Science Teacher's Book of Lists

**Frances Bartlett Barhydt, M.A. and
Paul W. Morgan, Ph.D.**

Paperback / 528 pages / 2002
ISBN: 0-13-793381-9

For science teachers at all levels, this unique information source gives you an unparalleled, all-in-one reference tool packed with information and ideas that will save you hours of research and preparation time and help you enliven and enrich both the teaching and learning of science. You'll gain over 290 lists related to life, chemical, physical, meteorological, earth and space science for use in creating instructional materials and planning lessons. Included are lists of scientific terms, generalizations, theories, laws, formulas, symbols, abbreviations, conversion charts, and more—all printed in a full-page format for easy photocopying and use.

Frances Barhydt has more than thirty years of teaching experience at the elementary, junior high, and university levels. She is currently a part-time faculty member of Lyndon State College and is Director of the Vermont Energy Education Program. She is the author of *Science Discovery Activities Kit* (The Center for Applied Research in Education, 1989) and coauthor of a number of teacher resource manuals, including *BUZ: A Hands-on Energy Education Program*. Mrs. Barhydt also works as an elementary science education consultant.

Paul Morgan is a retired Senior Research Fellow of the Dupont Company. He has received numerous awards for his professional work, including DuPont's Lavoisier Medal in 1992 for Technical Achievement. He is a Life Fellow of the Franklin Institute and was elected to the National Academy of Engineering.

Other Books of Interest

Janice VanCleave's A+ Projects in Biology: Winning Experiments for Science Fairs and Extra Credit

Janice VanCleave

Paperback / 224 pages / 2002
ISBN: 0-471-58628-5

Are you having a hard time coming up with a good idea for the science fair? Do you want to earn extra credit in your biology class? Or do you just want to know how the world really works? *Janice VanCleave's A+ Projects in Biology* can help you, and the best part is it won't involve any complicated or expensive equipment. This step-by-step guide explores 30 different topics and offers dozens of experiment ideas. The book also includes charts, diagrams, and illustrations. Here are just a few of the topics you'll be investigating: • Seed germination • Chromatography • Food preservatives • Cellular respiration • Operant conditioning. You'll be amazed at how easy it is to turn your own ideas into winning science fair projects. Also available: *Janice VanCleave's A+ Projects in Chemistry*.

Janice VanCleave won the Phi Delta Outstanding Teacher of the Year Award in 1982. She is a well-known presenter at schools, museums, and science fairs, and the author of fourteen other science experiment books.